MW00759538

Romanticism and Civilization

Politics, Literature, & Film

Series Editor
Lee Trepanier, Saginaw Valley State University

The Politics, Literature, & Film series is an interdisciplinary examination of the intersection of politics with literature and/or film. The series is receptive to works that use a variety of methodological approaches, focus on any period from antiquity to the present, and situate their analysis in national, comparative, or global contexts. Politics, Literature, & Film seeks to be truly interdisciplinary by including authors from all the social sciences and humanities, such as political science, sociology, psychology, literature, philosophy, history, religious studies, and law. The series is open to both American and non-American literature and film. By putting forth bold and innovative ideas that appeal to a broad range of interests, the series aims to enrich our conversations about literature, film, and their relationship to politics.

Recent Titles

Romanticism and Civilization: Love, Marriage, and Family in Rousseau's Julie, by Mark Kremer

Aldous Huxley: The Political Thought of a Man of Letters, by Alessandro Maurini

Sinclair Lewis and American Democracy, by Steven Michels

Liberty, Individuality, and Democracy in Jorge Luis Borges, by Alejandra M. Salinas

The Politics of Perfection: Technology and Creation in Literature and Film, by Kimberly Hurd Hale

Romanticism and Civilization

Love, Marriage, and
Family in Rousseau's Julie

Mark Kremer

LEXINGTON BOOKS
Lanham • Boulder • New York • London

Published by Lexington Books
An imprint of The Rowman & Littlefield Publishing Group, Inc.
4501 Forbes Boulevard, Suite 200, Lanham, Maryland 20706
www.rowman.com

Unit A, Whitacre Mews, 26-34 Stannary Street, London SE11 4AB

British Library Cataloguing in Publication Information Available

Library of Congress Cataloging-in-Publication Data Available

ISBN 978-1-4985-2747-7 (cloth : alk. paper)
ISBN 978-1-4985-2748-4 (electronic)

♾™ The paper used in this publication meets the minimum requirements of American National Standard for Information Sciences Permanence of Paper for Printed Library Materials, ANSI/NISO Z39.48-1992.

Printed in the United States of America

Contents

Contents

Preface

The return to the origins of romanticism in *Julie* is made necessary by the crisis of modern civilization. That crisis is inherent to modern civilization and was examined with unsurpassed clarity by Rousseau. He appropriated the word "bourgeois" to encapsulate all that civilization meant, and he gave it a precise meaning and a comprehensive articulation. The word has since been cheapened by Marx to mean the commercial class, and Rousseau certainly included them in his criticisms, but he had a profound understanding of civilization as a kind of nihilism that goes well beyond the simplicity of Marx's economic concerns and class strife. Marx himself and his proletariat would be bourgeois according to Rousseau, since the anticommercial intellectuals and even the anarchists are just part of the bourgeois nihilistic subculture. They belong to modern civilization, are a part of the urban landscape, and have no genius to found any meaningful new alternative. They, too, are nihilists caught in the web of modern life. For Rousseau, the term bourgeois captures an entire society from top to bottom. Romanticism means there is no going forward, but only a longing for the past, whether it be the ancient city, savage man, and, of course, the most attractive and realistic possibility for modern man—the romantic longing for love, marriage, and family.

Modern civilization is the effect of the Enlightenment. Civilization is defined by the progress of the sciences and the arts and always accompanies a softening of morals through commerce, luxury, idleness, and pleasures; but modern civilization, as distinct from ancient civilization, has the added feature of being part of the modern scientific project. This means that modern man is more grounded in science and equality than was ancient man. Ancient Athens could still put Socrates to death and it had no principle of equality, because it was not founded upon the idea of modern science. The modern scientific project gives to civilization a peculiar character. Science is both abstract and materialistic, and this character penetrates all aspects of modern life. Like science, modern man is cosmopolitan. He has been uprooted from his historical and sentimental traditions of religion, family, and country. He is a citizen of the world. His connection to humanity is abstract. He cannot possibly love it and cannot possibly fulfill any duties to it. Being obliged to everyone, he is obliged to no one and is in consequence of no consequence. He is nothing and is nowhere.

The Enlightenment had tried to bring science and humanity together through an alliance of power and utility, but neither is satisfactory by itself, nor taken together. Science does provide a degree of freedom by liberating man from a darkness worse than ignorance, and it flatters man's pride by giving him the self-sufficiency to stride the universe; but what is still more difficult is for man to return to himself in order to understand his own duties and end. Science is only preparatory to this task. It cannot say anything about man as man, and it ends where human consciousness begins. Science is a blind giant rather than human, and it maintains its justification in relation to the human only by being useful. Since science cannot justify any human life, it allies itself with the most powerful and the most general human passion (the desire for self-preservation), which by virtue of being powerful and general, requires little in the way of self-justification. Thought becomes abstract and life becomes living for the sake of living.

This combination of science and general utility is given political expression in the great liberal Enlightenment thinkers, Locke in particular, whom Rousseau treated as the most influential and successful of them all. In Locke, civilization becomes a social contract modeled after the business contract. The social contract is in turn derived from the conditions and interests of the state of nature, which is modeled after the scientific understanding of nature. Following the scientific model, Locke abstracts human beings from their connections to anything outside of their individual selves. The self is prior to the family and to country and there is no soul. The self, however, is not unique but a general self, defined by the general desire for self-preservation and the rights which secure it. The social order is an artifice, a contract, similar to a business contract where parties through enlightened self-interest discover an intersection of interests. Man is, therefore, an individual living in society. He obeys the laws because his reason tells him they are necessary for securing his own preservation, but he has no love of fatherland and even his attachment to family is secondary to his attachment to himself. Enlightenment means recognizing the rights related to preservation—life, liberty, and property, as belonging to man as man, and understanding that the respect for these rights joins individual desire to obedience to law. These are men's birthrights and it is in the modern liberal state that they are secured. Through rational calculation, the individual desires of nature and social obedience are united without the duties of either religion or of country.

Where Locke found a solution to the relation of nature to society, Rousseau found a problem. Rousseau recognized that civilization ameliorated national and religious hatreds, but if there is more tolerance, there is also less love and dutifulness. If civilization is less warlike, it is more degraded. If it is less given to the tyranny of force, it is more given to the tyranny of pleasures. If it is free from traditional prejudices, it has the prejudices of philosophic relativism, more dangerous to the freedom of the mind than religion itself. If there is liberation from the love of one's own, the attachment to humanity is abstract and the love of money is real. The individual living in society is a fiction, who belongs neither to himself, nor to society. As an individual he thinks of himself first, but as a member of society he conforms to public opinion and looks to others in order to form an opinion of himself. The individual living in society faces neither the harshness of being alone, nor the demands of community and is, therefore, both without character and beneath the issues of life. In Rousseau's words, he is a "nothing."

It gets worse. Eventually, the idea of political rights and the economic model of the social contract become too harsh for civilization. When Enlightenment civilization has progressed to the point of no longer being under duress from harsh necessities, it becomes too soft for war and punishment. It becomes increasingly less political and militaristic and increasingly more urban. This is its ultimate degradation and, in so many ways, the end of liberty. Here the language of rights is moved out of politics and into erotic and familial relations. Public life loses the stern language of justice, and instead adopts the language of politeness. The goal is to make sure that no one is offended. The knowledge of the art and of the rules of politeness replace the honesty and virtue of the citizen. Politeness is both a form of falseness and a form of conformity constituting a new form of civilizational tyranny. The women, seeing that men are no longer men and will not go to war, no longer see any reason why they should remain women. The military duties, which barred women from public life and the same rights with men, are no longer a barrier, so women leave the household and enter into public life, but they can only do so by transforming public life into a new form of tyranny — gynaecocracy.

Political life and domestic life become inverted in order to destroy the character and obligations of each. The hard life of men, and especially the military life, is impossible for women to follow so they must turn men into women. Where love rules, women rule. In the gynaecocracy, the women extend the power they have over their lovers, to the entire country. A youth culture rules, dominated by fashionable young girls, who become the new preceptors for society, teaching compassion for the world. Society itself becomes a homogeneous herd conforming to the rules of polite morality, while each really just seeks his own advantage. Universal compassion is impossible, so there really is no public duty. The polite morality of universal compassion is only part of the mix that sets the tone of society; sex and ridicule are more fundamental ingredients. Without the former, the men could not be effeminated and without the latter, the sexual empire would be subject to shame. Having given up their modesty, there can be no pride in virtue or even decency, and consequently false politeness, pretentious morality, and above all ridiculing those who would shame them become the motley dish of the urban tyranny.

While politics becomes love of the world, private relations are a state of war requiring either domination or self-protection through contract. Since love, marriage, and family have become only abstract and conditional relations, rights must be asserted against one another. Each is free to dissolve the private bonds as they will; there are no inviolable duties and no eternal loves. The name of wife and mother is no longer respected, and it is an embarrassment for a woman to be seen taking care of her own children, for it is a sign that she either cannot afford a nanny or that she is not free. The most honored woman is no longer the one about whom the least said, but the actress who is seen the most, of whom the most is seen, and by virtue of which is entitled to judge everything. Both sexes are degraded by the free and easy intermingling of the sexes from which emerges endless meaningless affairs. Ultimately, the herd with its surface politeness and its coarse pleasures is the final act before a stronger and harder people conquer them.

While Locke addresses himself to sexuality and procreation, he drains them of their meaning. He assumes that man has a duty to continue the species, which means that parents have a duty to preserve their children and educate them to the point where they can preserve themselves. Locke believes a two parent family is necessary to fulfill these parental duties, and, therefore, women owe their children a father. Naturally, the woman is the domestic being belonging to the household. She is free to choose her husband and can divorce once the child has been raised to the age of majority, but she is destined to domestic life by the need to continue the species. Locke believed that he had brought together a scientific view of sexuality, procreation, and preservation (both of the individual and of the species) into accord with man's social life, but Rousseau finds it contrived and problematic. Locke assumes that man will become a father before he becomes a husband, but why would he undertake the responsibilities of fatherhood after he has received the pleasures of a lover? Locke never took seriously the promiscuous and dangerous character of desire, because he was so far from really believing in the primacy of the individual in the state of nature that he presumed families. He wanted to soften them and democratize them to bring them more into accord with natural affection, as well as with natural freedom and equality, but he assumes their existence.

Locke was correcting both Aristotle's political understanding of republicanism and its corresponding understanding of the family. Like Aristotle, Locke subordinates sexuality to his politics, but whereas Locke is liberal and democratic, Aristotle looks to the common good and is aristocratic. Aristotle argued that women are not slaves, and he even went so far as to define barbarism as the treatment of women as slaves. He recognizes friendship in marriage and families, though they are not the highest kinds of friendship because they share too much in inequality and their ends are connected to the body and utility. Aristotle even emphasizes the need for the education of women and blames the lack of it for the destruction of Sparta. Yet, for Aristotle, female freedom and republican freedom cannot coincide, because the female cannot enjoy her freedom under the strict demands of republican politics. Her freedom is simply in conflict with politics and the family, and her liberty finds an affinity with tyranny and foreign influence. By nature, she would use her freedom to expand her empire, and that means the end of the discipline and order required for republicanism.

Like Locke, Montesquieu softened politics and the family with liberalism, but Montesquieu thought that Locke was still too harsh. If gynaecocracy has a philosopher, it is Montesquieu. His is a liberal politics without the harshness of theory and principle. There is no overly harsh state of nature from which to derive a social contract, and there are not even natural rights or even a doctrine of freedom and equality. Certainly, there is no right to revolution as in Locke and no doctrine of sovereignty. All of this is too full of political spirit. Even the commercial spirit present in Locke is softened in Montesquieu. Whereas Locke writes about labor and private property, Montesquieu encourages luxury and counts fashion and its attendant vanities as an important part of the commercial republic. He even embraces what we would call multiculturalism and he takes much of the moral strength out of the law by understanding it in terms of material, abstract, and historical causes.

Rousseau's politics do not suit his novel about private life. It is true that his politics and his novel have something in common to the extent that both are opposed to modern civilization, but when asked why he did not sign his name to the novel with his usual title "Citizen of Geneva," Rousseau made clear that the romantic passions are one thing and the duties of a citizen quite another. The citizen is wholly devoted to his country. He is but a fraction belonging to a greater whole, the greatest and most extreme model being Sparta under the laws of Lycurgus. Rousseau makes no attempt to bring private life (love, marriage, and family) into accord with political life. They have different ends and perfections, and the attempt to make them accord would do justice to neither. The citizen is "denatured." His natural inclinations are subordinated to the common good and his duties require that he give up his life and those of his children for his country. Private life to the contrary, is in accord with the most immediate desires and attachments. For Rousseau, love is a form of self-knowledge and its claims and its gods need to be investigated independent of political ends. In a certain sense, the liberalism of Montesquieu resembles the patriarchies to which he was opposed, for although he freed sexuality from patriarchy, he made use of it for liberal politics and humanitarian ends—that is to say the softening of morals. Montesquieu saw that libertinism was not simply contrary to an orderly society, because easy sexual mores made man less fanatical and more tractable.

Rousseau tried to steer a course somewhere between Aristotle and the liberalism of Locke and of Montesquieu by treating love, marriage, and family as themselves possible communities. Burke even went so far as to attribute to *Julie* the distinction of being the single greatest cause of the French Revolution. The romantic orders cannot abide patriarchy. This means that the female takes center stage as in a gynaecocracy but their characters and their rule could not be more different. Rousseau argues that there is no honorable course or secure path for women once they have left the sphere of love, marriage, and family. In other words, the woman does not belong to herself and her freedom is within the sphere of private and domestic relations. This is where her honorable influence rests. She can rule outside that sphere through a culture of sex that weakens the male, but her rule would constitute a tyranny and, as everyone knows, tyranny degrades both the tyrant as well as the oppressed.

The romantic influence of the female accords with the natural differences between the sexes, rather than with an abstract scientific understanding or a democratic project. Simply put, the female is more dependent on the male by nature than is the male on the female. She is, therefore, more defined by her sex than is he and she lives more in relation to him than he does in relation to her. Biology counts. He is physically stronger, she carries the child and gives birth, the child by nature falls to her, and mating requires that she stimulate desire. Sexuality cannot be the same for both since she risks so much more in it. An impossible tyranny would be required to keep women from suffering from the inequalities related to sexual desire, so they must accommodate themselves to it. The gynaecocracy is the degrading accommodation and romanticism the honorable path. Women cannot command men and make them obey, because the first law of nature is the law of force, but they can make the stronger willingly serve the weaker. This is the prudent path, since there is no other. If the man is to serve, the woman must please. If she resents this, it is a resentment against nature and against her own sex, and not due to any injustice of men. In order to please she must be modest. Modesty is her foundational virtue upon which all the others are built. It must accompany her always, even in the act itself. The intermingling of wills gives love its charm, and modesty by creating doubt, makes love possible. Modesty covers with love and decency an inherently indecent act. It is the inner awareness that the sexes are directed toward one another and have claims upon one another. Modesty is nature's guile and woman's virtue that informs desire with admiration and a tender and exclusive attachment. In this sense, romanticism is more civilized than civilization.

While the male needs the female for his desire, the female needs the male for both her desires and her needs. Modesty promises fidelity, and by allowing the male to make a claim upon her, she makes a claim upon him. Not only must the female be virtuous but she must also maintain the reputation for virtue. This is sometimes said to be an unfair double standard but it has its cause in nature. The fair sex depends upon the empire of opinion more than the male, precisely because the male is by nature more independent and belongs more to himself. The concern for reputation is a weakness in him, whereas for a woman it is a necessary part of her honor. Since she is the one in greater need, she is in greater need of approval. In order to love, one must make oneself loveable and this includes a concern for reputation. Modesty and reputation are a kind of female wisdom that recognize the place in which nature has placed women in relation to men. Nature demands the continuity of the species and she must submit to desire, but she must be honored, loved, and served willingly, which means that the submission to desire must always remain ambiguous and a man must never be sure if she submits to his desire or to his will and strength. Love means dependency, and whoever wishes to remain free and independent while having love, will have neither. This is the situation of civilization. Free and independent human beings can contract with one another but they cannot love. They will have neither the sentiments, nor the virtues required for it and consequently sexuality, which is a source of the sweetest sentiments, must become mutual exploitation. This cannot but weigh more heavily on women than on men. Locke's idea of the state of nature and the social contract threaten the psychological subtlety and self-understanding necessary for relations of modesty. He prepares women for freedom and equality, but insists on their domesticity without honoring and romanticizing the domestic life.

A similar problem of subordinating private life to ends outside of it can be seen in Christianity to which Rousseau draws our attention through the subtitle of his novel. La nouvelle Héloïse must be juxtaposed to the old Héloïse or one might say the medieval Héloïse. This famous tale of love between Héloïse Argenteuil and Peter Abelard is a tragic one. It is a romance between two high born and educated youths. Both are accomplished in philosophy and letters, but neither of their educations legitimate their passions. Their science is abstract and their religion forbidding. Without getting into the well-known details of their tragic history, Abelard renounces his love in the name of Christianity and as a monk exhorts Héloïse, who is cloistered as a nun, to give up her passion for him and to direct it toward God, for they are now brother and sister under the same father. As a philosopher, Aberlard was responsible for Christian-Aristotelianism or the use of Aristotle, and especially his logic, to support Christianity. He moderated faith and made it more open to reason and less reliant on revelation, but neither his philosophy, nor his religion left a place for romantic love. Héloïse's undying love for Abelard both elevated and degraded her. She declared that she would rather be his whore than his wife, and her son, whom in the admiration for science she named Astrolabe, was a matter of near indifference to her. She dies unable to conquer, even consumed by, a desperate love that is unrequited and has no force and no nobility other than her devotedness. Her extensive studies have no relation to either her love for Abelard or to her connection to her son, and in the end turn out to be nothing more than sophistication. Ultimately, it is their love for which they are both remembered and not their learning, demonstrating that love can be examined as an ideal of its own, and deserves its own mating of philosophy and religion. This means that there is need for a new Abelard in addition to a new Héloïse, and that the Aristotelian-Christian tradition is as inadequate as the Baconian-liberal tradition.

Romanticism is, of course, a mating of philosophy and of religion on the bed of nature. Rousseau's Abelard (St. Preux) is a Platonist. Aristotle looked at sexuality as just another passion that needed to be regulated by virtue. As fear is regulated by courage, sexual desire is regulated by moderation. Self-control is necessary to Aristotle, and the pride we feel in it is natural. There is, therefore, no romantic love in Aristotle. Plato is the philosopher for lovers according to Rousseau, and what this means is that Plato took sexuality seriously as a source of self-knowledge. But even Platonic love is unsatisfactory for the romantic Rousseau, because the highest expression of love for Plato is *eros*, which is philosophy. The love of wisdom is an unrequited love and ultimately one that is not enthusiastic and inspired, and certainly not sexual. So although Plato took sexuality seriously, it culminates in philosophy, whereas Rousseau uses philosophy to support love, marriage, and family. For Rousseau, sentiment or feeling as distinct from reason and philosophy informs nature.

With respect to religion, Julie is a Christian but she does not believe in hell, and her heaven is a promise to one day be reunited with her lover, whom she had to give up in life, to marry Wolmar, an Epicurean atheist, converted to belief by her death, and the friend of her father. Her conflict is not one of body and soul but a romantic conflict between her love and her marriage. Romantic love cannot but be more free than the marital and familial order. Julie does not choose her husband because she could not become a wife and a mother by abandoning and killing her own father. This does not mean that Rousseau defends patriarchy, as is clear from the nature of the tragedy and the creation of a new familial order with Wolmar at its head, but he makes clear that love, marriage, and family are not a simple unity.

Medieval romance is gallantry. Rousseau says that the foundation for knighthood and its respect for God and women was the barbarism of warriors, who traveled with their women. Chivalry belongs to this barbarism and the feudal ages which emerged from it. The gallantry and coquetry of Paris are the empty forms of these relations stripped of their political and religious orders. Rousseau saw that there was need for a new understanding of romance given the end of the medieval orders and the advance of civilization. There were great novelists before him who undertook that task, Prévost and Richardson being the most important. Of Richardson's *Clarissa*, Rousseau declared it to be the greatest novel ever written, but neither Prévost, nor Richardson are adequate guides in the new world. They naturalized the spirituality of Christianity and moderated the authority of the feudal order, but they still wrote for a world dominated by Christianity and aristocracy. While it is true that *Manon Lescaut*, *Pamela*, and *Clarissa* recognize the force of romance and therewith the ascendency of the female, they do not adequately grasp the revolutions that were about to bring the medieval ages to a complete end. The novels of Prévost and Richardson share the taste for the chivalrous and the saintly. While Prévost is sentimental and Richardson inspires admiration for virtue, they are unable to found their romances on a natural love. Rousseau's romantic hero is a commoner who falls in love with a girl of noble birth, whereas Richardson's commoner is a woman elevated by the high birth of her lover; and Prévost's *Manon* is still a story of a sinner who becomes a saint. Rousseau turned away from Christian piety and aristocratic patriarchy to sentiment, and in particular those romantic sentiments supported by nature. This was his great innovation in both philosophy and art. The romantic taste gave new life to a new kind of love—both sincere and full of longing it was meant as a correction to civilization's falseness and coarseness. Through sentiment, Rousseau believed he had recovered the beauty and sweetness of life.

Let us end with some final reflections on Rousseau and Plato, as well as on the fate of Romanticism. Rousseau refers to Plato as the philosopher for lovers, and he openly imitated Socrates by presenting himself as both the perfection and bad conscience of civilization. Like Socrates, he took morality more seriously than the scientists and sophists, not because he was a conventional moralist, but because he saw that the investigation of morality was a path back to man—a way of fulfilling the Delphic command to know thyself. Modern civilization cannot take this command seriously any more than could the pre-socratic philosophers and sophists. Advanced civilization satisfies neither the demands of political virtue, nor the requirements of wisdom and, therefore, there is a need to examine the perfection of both and their conflicts. Bacon's science fiction is a monstrosity of science and mass humanity, and like any monster, it is insensitive to the questions of virtue and happiness. Rousseau took seriously man's longing for wholeness and eternity, and he exposed the abstractness and coarseness of sham globalism and scientific progress. The popularization of reason is the death of philosophy, for it becomes just a prejudice in favor of progress. Although Rousseau is in agreement with Plato in opposition to enlightenment, Rousseau condemned dialectics, and his return to the past is not a myth of anamnesis but one of sentiment. Julie is a substitute for Socrates, and it is through the female rather than the philosopher that Rousseau forms new communities. He does this because, paradoxically, he agrees with a certain aspect of the Enlightenment—that nature is body and that therefore all forms of community depend upon the imagination. Sexuality and procreation in particular are those aspects of body most readily, that is to say most naturally, connected to imagination and to the wills of others. For Plato, philosophy must subordinate to reason both poetic imagination and the passions they flatter, whereas Rousseau perfects reason with sentiment.

Rousseau turned to Plato not as a philosopher but as a poet of the divine. Through the various kinds of affection for Julie (as lover, as friend, as daughter, as mother, and as wife) private life is revealed to be a place of the strongest connections and deepest meanings. The struggle between reason and religion plays itself out on this stage with new romantic gods emerging for the different romantic relations. Man and woman have complimentary natures, and their wills can be directed toward a common end without either the subjugation of the female or the gynaecocratic enslavement of the male. Private life needs to be supported by a teleological explanation of sexuality and gender in the face of scientific determinism and democratic indeterminateness. The love that forms around Julie, is made up of a commoner, an aristocrat, and a king. The political classes are not artificially leveled by a doctrine of equality or by any abstract humanity, but coalesce around a woman they love and admire, just as Socrates' admirers did with him.

Julie ou La Nouvelle Heloise is of course a kind of gentle tragedy consistent with romantic tenderness, as Socrates' end is consistent with the gentleness of philosophy. Julie is unable to reconcile her love for St. Preux, her obligations to her father, and her gratitude and affections for her husband. She dies saving her youngest son from drowning, but it is really a kind of suicide. Tormented by her heart, she seeks death. The conflicts and ideals of private life dominated literature after *Julie* for more than a century, and really only came to an end with Tolstoy. Artists dedicated themselves to the fate of love and family in the modern world, and found a compelling tale in the struggles of the human heart and the psychology of men and women. All of this provided an oasis of fresh water in what Rousseau called the mud of urban existence. As an artistic movement inspiring the tone of life and even the ideals of nations, Romanticism had a short life. It still reverberates on a personal level through novels which continue to attract. Austen and Tolstoy remain popular even though the lifeblood at their source has largely been forgotten, but they are entertainments and fantasies as distinct from artistic models that inform life. The romantic taste was meant to be a refined and rare taste informed by philosophy, poetry, and religion, and it was hoped that it could somehow always remain a touchstone to which one could return amidst the vulgarity and emptiness of modern civilization.

The waning influence of romanticism is in part to be attributed to the coarsening of modern sensibilities accompanied by lack of learning. Commenting on how far man has fallen, Rousseau says that his characters astound us just for having the virtues of their sex. The refined feelings and moral astuteness of Julie are all but incomprehensible in our sewers. But Romanticism also faltered on account of its own inner conflicts. Rousseau was aware of these conflicts and even delighted in pointing them out. It is not clear why devotion to love is admirable if it is an illusion. If the true nature of sexuality is bodily, while the romantic is imaginary, then why not science and hedonism instead of poetry? Rousseau did not leave much to stand on. To all thinking and serious human beings, he had discredited the Enlightenment, but he had also discredited his alternatives with the possible exception of nature, which became ever so problematic and inhuman. While he believed that science conflicted with life because it saw life from the outside, he never believed that the scientific understanding of nature was untrue. In this one respect, this great opponent of Enlightenment was its most faithful follower. Convinced that nature is body, he went further than all before him and denied that reason was natural to man and, therewith, that the human itself is historical rather than natural. His understanding of nature is a thinking through of the materialism of science to its end, and like an inverse Plato, he ultimately sought for a wholeness in nature, but of the animal kind instead of the divine. His genius was in the recovery of human life from the reductionism of science. He articulated man's consciousness and his manifold experiences with a fullness rivalling any poet, and the best who came after him had nothing to add. And yet, paradoxically, by accepting the scientific understanding of nature and following it through to its most extreme and logical conclusion, he might have been led astray by science more than anyone.

Acknowledgments

This book was written by a young man and student in search of himself. I chose to write on Rousseau's *Julie* because it was recognized as the foundation of Romanticism and as the modern rival to Plato's *Symposium*. The fate of love in the modern world was Rousseau's great theme. He believed that no people could be truly civilized if they did not know love, no matter how tolerant and averse to cruelty, and so he hit the Achilles' heel of modern man, who prides himself on his civility but whose private relations are course and sterile. The Parisians, who were supposed to be a model of love, had no heart. They were in reality only gallants and coquettes hiding their course desires under the veneer of politeness. They knew vanity and sensuality but none of the religiosity of love, which demands sacrifices from its votaries. Rousseau's lovers live in a small village at the foot of the Swiss Alps. They are educated without being sophisticates. Their study of philosophy and of poetry, unlike their counterparts in the city, are animated by a genuine need for self-understanding that seeks to both honor and justify their love. They are less interested in challenging authorities than they are with the meaning of their feelings and substance of their thoughts. In Paris, books are abstract, vain and frivolous entertainments with no relation to life. Their tone is one of criticism because their readers have no experience of love and virtue, and only a taste for derision. *Julie* is, therefore, a book not only about lovers, but also a book about books. It is a book that seeks legitimate sexual expression without reducing sexuality to either a dumb instinct or to arbitrary choice. In this sense, it is a book at odds with both our science and our relativism. Modern man has no need for poetry because he is animated by fears and interests, rather than love of the beautiful. I was fortunate enough to work with teachers who understood the importance of books and allowed me to live with this one. Romanticism had come to be seen through the eyes of feminism as not only unjust, but as an enemy of unquestioned democratic progress. Love was not to be trusted and honored but exposed as a form of oppression in a power struggle between men and women. Feminism, though in no way puritanical, found itself in the role of persecutor masquerading as savior, and male sexual desire, or at least the kind directed toward women, became sinful again. This new tyranny against nature and its accompanying degradations are discussed by Rousseau in *Julie*, but he did not want to destroy the effect of his novel by concentrating excessively on what is bad, so he wrote only a handful of terse letters explaining the character and causes of gynaecocracy in Paris. I originally wrote on those letters in my dissertation and slightly expanded them into a journal article shortly afterward, but only recently published separately, under the title "Cosmopolitanism as Nihilism: Rousseau's Study of Paris" in *Perspectives on Political Science*, v.45, 2016, pp. 32–46. The article makes no substantial changes from the original, and here I have borrowed from it to slightly modify the original. Nothing would be gained by a comparison as they essentially make the same points and argument. I thank Taylor & Francis for permission to use the article in part and in whole.

Introduction

La Nouvelle Héloïse is the most influential novel ever written. It shares with the *Social Contract* the honor of inspiring the French Revolution and, to a lesser extent, German idealism, but it stands alone as the fountainhead of romanticism. It is a celebration and critical examination of love and family.

Rousseau's romanticism seems to pile contradiction upon contradiction. It complicates even more the confusion created by his conflicting praise of both the self-contained independence of natural man and the selfless patriotism of the citizen by adding a third alternative: the lover or spouse. Yet, what seems at first to be a bewildering contradiction is really a helpful piece of the puzzle. Love and family are a mixture of the extreme naturalness of primitive man and the extreme sociality of the citizen. They are social relations requiring a common good, but are clearly built around and joined together by the pleasures of intercourse and procreation, rather than painful acts of war and punitive legislation. The contradictory elements of Rousseau's thought are actually human possibilities that attempt to solve the problem of man's dividedness by making him whole.

The dividedness to which Rousseau sought a solution is also a human type. Rousseau called him the bourgeois. The bourgeois is a consequence of the Enlightenment. He is the result of the application of modern science to society. His dividedness reveals an unbearable conflict between truth and life for which Rousseau seeks a solution. Natural science teaches that there is no possibility of community, because the real is the body, and the body individuates. Yet, civil man must live with other human beings. This conflict is a formula for hypocrisy. Not only is the bourgeois incapable of a real concern for the public good, but he cannot even be consistently concerned with his own good. He will sacrifice his own good and interests for the sake of praise. He lives neither for himself, nor for others. Rousseau characterizes such half-hearted persons as nothing. To be something means to be whole. It means to be all private body or all devotion to the common good, or to be a harmonious mixture of the two. To be all body is to be primitive. To be all devotion to the common good is to be a citizen; and, to be a harmonious mixture of these two extremes is to live a life of private attachments. Such attachments are more within reach for modern man than the two extremes. There is no possibility of simply returning to primitive man, and those who try to do so on the

1

level of civilization are rare because they must be independent of human opinion. As for the citizen, Christianity and the Enlightenment have made the idea of the fatherland almost incomprehensible. Their other worldliness and individualism, respectively, leave no place for the attachment to country and the love of the common good. Love and family are the most practical alternatives for modern man.

The hypocrisy that arises from the division between nature and society is seen not only in contradictions between natural inclination and the need to satisfy one's vanity, but also in the conflict between thought and life. Science and the health of civil man are in conflict with one another. Most humans cannot live in the world as science understands it. According to science, man is a bodily composition that will decompose; he has no nature different from the nonhuman things. Everything man loves is body on its way to nothing. Most men, however, rebel against imagining the decay and disintegration of what they love. It is too ugly to look upon. Thus, their sentiments and passions are never brought into harmony with their science. The bourgeois, however, is a hypocrite, not only because his sentiments and his passions are not brought into accord with his thoughts, but also because his thought is not brought into accord with his sentiments and his passions. The bourgeois accumulates wealth as if he were to live forever, but he does not believe in immortality, and he seeks the honor and praise of others, even though he does not believe in the possibility of community. His thought is only partially connected to his life. He is in so much contradiction with himself and his opinion about nature that he cannot even have an opinion about what he is. He is absurd, or (what amounts to the same thing) nothing.

The bourgeois' conflict between himself and others, as well as his conflict between life and death, has its theoretical roots in liberalism, according to Rousseau. He traces the incoherencies of bourgeois life to the peculiar failures of Hobbes and Locke to find their way back to nature. He considers their thought to be an unsatisfactory combination of nature and society, which are formulas for the bourgeois because they satisfy neither natural selfishness nor the social demands of justice. Rousseau's analysis of the inadequacy of their thought concentrates on two essential elements of nature and society, death and sex. He concentrates on Hobbes with respect to death, and Locke with respect to intercourse and procreation.

Hobbes' state of nature is premised on the insight that man is an asocial animal, that his selfish passions are more fundamental than any of his attachments to others. But Hobbes attributes to man in the state of nature characteristics that presuppose society. He attributes to him the fear of violent death and the desire for vainglory. These are passions that require the use of a developed imagination—an imagination that can call images to mind at will and that must, therefore, be accompanied by self-consciousness.[1] The development of the imagination, however, requires language and reason, because speech is necessary for general ideas, and general ideas are, in turn, necessary for the ability to recall images at will; and, since speech is a mode of communication, it presupposes sociality. Hobbes did not think through the premise that man is by nature asocial. He mistook antisociality for asociality.

If reason is in the service of the asocial passions by nature, as Hobbes presumes, then man must be stripped of all the passions that depend on reason in order to discover his nature. Hobbes did not do this. His failure to think through man's asociality leads him to an understanding of life that is an unsatisfactory mixture of passion and reason. Hobbes places "in the first place a general inclination of all mankind, a perpetual and restless desire of power after power,that ceaseth only in death."[2] Reason is a calculative tool that helps man to gain the power to satisfy his deepest desire—the desire to preserve himself. Rousseau thinks this interplay between reason and passion is a kind of madness that fails to understand properly both natural passion and society. Rousseau opposes Hobbes by returning to the ideas of wholeness and contentment. He finds, in animal nature, something more fundamental than the restless desire for power after power. The desire for the power to preserve oneself presupposes that existence is pleasant. The sentiment of existence is a complete satisfaction that affirms the goodness of life.[3] It precedes reason in that it is oblivious to the past and the future; its immersion in the present is haunted by neither fears, nor hopes. The sentiment of existence is definitive of man's presocial nature.

Civil man, on the other hand, cannot have the immediate contentment characteristic of man in the state of nature. But the character of desire requires that he be restored to himself, if only through the promise of a state of complete satisfaction. All desire that is not immediate—bodily desire—requires the promise of a permanent state of satisfaction in order to sustain itself. It is this understanding of desire that makes Rousseau's rhetoric so searing. He speaks of women who perform a useless act over and over again; and he ridicules wealthy gluttons, who go to so much trouble to eat what they will pass the next morning. It is not the nature of desire to be unlimited, for limitlessness undoes desire. Rousseau conceives of reason, therefore, not as a tool of desire, but as a power (although a very weak power limited to a few) for limiting desire. Love, marriage, and family are important themes for him because they give meaning to sexual desire by placing limitations upon it, although those limitations are not simply the work of reason.

Hobbes neither got back to nature, nor attempted to restore civilized man to his lost wholeness because he looked to nature to solve the problems of his time rather than the permanent human problems. Hobbes' thought is directed against the horrors of war, especially religious wars and civil wars. He is concerned with the establishment of a legitimate central authority that can maintain civil order among factions. His state of nature is an untenable combination of nature and society because it is an ad hoc construction that is meant to point directly to his doctrine of sovereignty. Rousseau goes so far as to call him an apologist for the monarchy.[4]

Hobbes' attempt to give direction to life by concentrating the imagination on fear of violent death is a form of social and rational optimism that fails to address the human situation. By turning the imagination toward violent death at the hands of other men, Hobbes directs the mind to solving problems through social arrangements. Death, as a simple fact of nature, is not part of his thought. His attempt to preserve humanity from the brutality of force through a teaching of justice fails to protect humanity from the animality of a safe, but meaningless, existence. Hobbes cannot find any meaning other than peaceful coexistence, because he does not address himself to the problem of man's end—to his mortality. The necessity of death means that self-preservation cannot be the fundamental passion, because it is a desire that clearly has no hope of being satisfied. The mortality of the body makes living for oneself, especially in the narrow sense of one's breathing existence, a problem. Yet, one cannot live for anything beyond oneself in Hobbes' civil society because it presents itself as an aggregate of individuals forming an artificial legal body. Hobbes did not have the intransigence necessary to think through the distinction between nature and society because he did not address himself to the meaning of death for life.

Rousseau also criticizes Locke's unsatisfactory combination of nature and society. He takes aim at Locke's attempt to build civil society, especially the family, on nature. At the beginning of Book V of *Emile*, Rousseau says that Locke ends the education of a gentleman where it ought to begin—with his erotic education.[5] This criticism must be understood in combination with note (l) of *The Second Discourse* where Rousseau takes issue with Locke's understanding of the genesis of the family.[6] According to Rousseau, Locke's failure to educate gentlemen in matters of love and marriage is the consequence of his hidden teleology. Locke argues that the sexes cohabit because of the desire to preserve the species. The male remains with the female in order to protect her in pregnancy and to help preserve the child until it can take care of itself.

Locke, however, fails to explain how the desire to preserve the species can be a conscious desire if man is by nature asocial. Furthermore, even if the desire for intercourse is nature's ruse that uses individual desire for the continuation of the species, there is still no reason for the male to remain with the female by nature after he is satisfied. According to Rousseau, Locke's confidence in nature blinds him to the task of educating the sexes for one another. This is Rousseau's colossal task and what clearly separates him from Enlightenment thought.

In opposition to Locke, Rousseau argues that men must become husbands before they become fathers. He traces the cohabitation between the sexes to the construction of permanent dwellings.[7] Since permanent dwellings, unlike caves, require repairs, they prepare the ground for a division of labor, one to gather and hunt, and one to fix the dwelling. It is private property in its most primitive form that is the seed for the family, not the desire to preserve the species. After being in the hut together for some time, man discovers himself a father, and then the primitive family is born.

According to Rousseau, Locke failed to think through the effects of his understanding of nature and justice on the relations between the sexes because he had an unjustified confidence in nature. The differentiation between the sexes, which Locke himself takes for granted, has no justification in nature or equality. A great deal of Rousseau's rhetoric and reasoning is devoted to differentiating the sexes and giving them a common good. His reasoning and rhetoric is directed against the idea of the free and equal relations between the sexes, which is a powerful prejudice in Paris and which gains support from the modern understanding of nature and equality. Rousseau openly addresses himself to the free and equal relations between the sexes in several places, but nowhere does he address himself to it more single-mindedly than in *The Letter to d'Alembert* and the beginning of Book V of *Emile*, where he introduces the education of Sophie.[8]

Rousseau's arguments were met with resistance by Enlightenment feminists, most notably Mary Wollstonecraft. In her *A Vindication of the Rights of Women*, she isolates Rousseau as a sensualist, whose differentiation of the sexes tyrannizes over women and debases both sexes. Her book is meant to lay the foundations for the esteem of women by arguing that they are the equals of the male, because they can partake in the universal dignity of human beings.[9] Through the cultivation of the faculty of reason, the female is free and virtuous, and pursues a human end independent of her sex. This cultivation, according to Wollstonecraft, will cause men to esteem her. Wollstonecraft, however, is not critical of women becoming mothers and wives. She hopes that the esteem given to women will simply change the nature of love, marriage, and family. These relations will be changed by making the female a friend in the highest sense of the term. The male and the female will esteem one another as beings in pursuit of and capable of knowledge.

Wollstonecraft was not the first woman who attempted to gain the esteem of men by proudly renouncing the virtues of her sex and proposing that men and women share one excellence. St. Preux makes mention of women who, having given up the virtues of their sex, try to imitate those of the male, and Rousseau addresses himself directly to the question. He says that he only knows of one female who was successful in imitating the virtues of the male, and that for all her virtue he would not find her attractive.[10] This criticism is decisive. Society requires procreation, and, therefore, attraction leading to intercourse. The virtue of the

female must not only make her estimable, but also pleasing. Wollstonecraft takes for granted what Rousseau does not, that men will continue to
want to be husbands and fathers, and that women will continue to want
to be wives and mothers, even though their virtue is unconnected to
these relations. Friendship does not require intercourse and procreation.
In fact, intercourse and procreation get in the way of friendship. Wollstonecraft throws the baby out with the bathwater. In order to correct and
guard against the degradation of sexual relations, she looks to a standard
of virtue that does not relate the male and the female through their sexuality. This is, of course, what Plato does in his *Republic*. But, Plato knew
he was abolishing love and family. Furthermore, Plato outlines what his
regime is and what it means to belong to it as a citizen. Wollstonecraft
does not do this. She is too caught up in the spirit of protest to give an
account of her new republic.

Both Plato and Wollstonecraft would have the sexes on a footing of
equal familiarity, while maintaining austere relations, even when having
intercourse. Plato's male and female warriors have intercourse for reasons of duty, and Wollstonecraft's male and female philosophers have
intercourse as part of their mutual admiration for one another. Rousseau
argues that the equality and familiarity between the sexes, far from accompanying austerity, will lead to promiscuity and the most intolerable
abuses. Wollstonecraft is aware that the enlightenment of women, familiarity, and equality between the sexes has its greatest example in Paris.
Yet, far from being a republic of philosophers, it is dissolute:

> In France, there is no doubt a more general diffusion of knowledge
> than in any part of the European world, and I attribute it, in a great
> measure, to the social intercourse between the sexes. . . . And modesty,
> the fairest garb of virtue! has been more grossly insulted in France than
> even in England, till their women have treated as prudish that attention
> to decency, which brutes instinctively observe.[11]

She does not think there is a necessary relation between equality, familiarity, enlightenment, and dissoluteness. Rousseau thought there was,
and he states his reasons. One might add that Rousseau thought he was
really of like mind with Plato on this question, since Plato is not, like
Wollstonecraft, in earnest about the equality of men and women, but
proposes it in order to show how incommensurate the mind is with political life.

Rousseau argues that equality accompanies promiscuity because
equality is inconsistent with modesty. The modesty of the female differ-
entiates the sexes and regulates sexual desire because it is accompanied
by an awareness of both love and morality. It is informed by the desire
for an exclusive and permanent attachment, and is, therefore, inconsistent with the pleasures of a hedonist and the indifference of a scientist. It
is no accident that Wollstonecraft argues against female modesty and

tries to replace it with a kind of intellectual modesty characteristic of both male and female.[12] Once modesty is abandoned there will not be a society of mutual esteem, but of mutual degradation because the fear and shame that controlled sexual desire will be removed. Furthermore, the female, finding herself unprotected by respect for the virtue of her sex and unable to imitate the virtues of the male, will seek power over him by making him effeminate. He will give up his freedom in order to enjoy her favors. Wollstonecraft is aware of the power of coquetry, and, like Rousseau, she despises it for degrading both sexes. Her mistake is in confusing coquetry with modesty. The sexual relations of her times were so debased that she turned against them all together. She, in fact, only contributes to the debasement by casting off female modesty and failing to give an account of responsible sexual relations.

One might ask why the female cannot be sexual and still imitate the male virtues. The reason is simple. The female risks far more in the act of intercourse than does the male.[13] She is weaker, and, due to anatomical necessity, can be raped, but cannot rape. Most important, she risks pregnancy. How can the sexes be the same with respect to an act, which does not contain equal risks? One might argue that commerce diminishes the difference with respect to risk. A wealthy female can support a child. Furthermore, birth control and abortion mean that pregnancy is not even a factor. But, society cannot do without the people reproducing themselves, and the general disorder caused by promiscuity among them is destructive to society as a whole.[14] The free and equal relations between the sexes is necessarily accompanied by the opinion that a mother does not need a father for her child, and is likely not to have one for it.[15] Paternal duties cannot be derived from an indeterminate act. The free and equal relations between the sexes are, therefore, terrible for the bulk of human beings who make up society and for society as a whole; they are the self-serving prejudices of the upper class, and Rousseau says as much. They are "the philosophy of a day which is born and dies in the corner of a big city and wishes to smother the cry of nature and the unanimous voice of humankind."[16]

Although the differences between the male and the female have a basis in biological necessity, those biological differences do not by nature legitimate their different virtues. Primitive man is asocial precisely because the female does not need the assistance of the male to bring the child to a state of independence. But, the dependency of civil man translates the biological differences into different ways of life. This is where Rousseau's disparate geniuses as a philosopher and a poet meet. The differentiation of the sexes not only must be a social necessity, but must be made beautiful and just. Those differences can be made legitimate only by creating an order of wills. The order of wills is not founded on authority or on abstract principle. The order of wills is found in a sweet union of complimentary virtues.

Rousseau creates love from sexual desire, imagination, and amour-propre. Love is determined by the female situation. Her situation is very simple. She must inflame desire and be subjected to its satisfaction, but she must always have an excuse for giving in.[17] Modesty allows her to do all this. Modesty inflames desire because it kindles the imagination. It places a barrier between the senses and, thereby, forces the imagination to substitute an image far more alluring than the senses could apprehend. It is, thus, that Rousseau finds the Spartan maidens, who dance nude at their festivals, to be more chaste than a Chinese girl, who extends her covered toe from beneath her gown.[18] The Spartans were so simple in their morals that the female body was not an object of fantasy.

Besides inflaming desire through the imagination, modesty mixes amour-propre with the senses. Clothing is not the only barrier to overcome. The male must gain the will of the female, and not only against other men, but, more importantly, against herself. She must submit to the bold audacity of the male, for nature demands it, but in the midst of submission there must be an ambiguity about her intention. The male must remain in doubt about whether he takes by strength or receives willingly. The ambiguity in the male's mind sweetens the pleasures of both with amour-propre. This is how both feel the charm of love and avoid the Scylla and Charybdis of force and sensual pleasure. The male senses his strength, but is charmed by the thought of being chosen, and the female feels her weakness, but is charmed by the thought of giving herself. These are not games, but necessary parts for a union that is permanent and sweet.

The differentiation of the sexes gains inward conviction from the sweet experience of love. Lover and beloved form a union, without the need of outside authority. But, these felt differences also require outward confirmations. They must believe that they are made for love. There must, therefore, be a teleology of the body, which apprehends a plan in sensual beauty. This is one of Rousseau's poetic achievements. He describes the female body in teleological terms, which affirm the virtue of modesty. Her skin is thinner and lighter than the male's, so that her blush can be seen. Her muscles are more supple because boldness and strength are unseemly in her. She runs more slowly so as to be caught in her flight. She is smaller and of more delicate feature because hard labor is not her task. She is inclined to chatter more than the male because she is inclined to learn the art of pleasing. Rousseau's description of the beauty of the female body abstracts from the harsh biological differences. He lends beauty to necessity and reason to sensuality.

Rousseau does more than analyze the theoretical problems at the root of the bourgeois and explain the psychological requirements for his romantic solutions. In *La Nouvelle Héloïse*, he portrays bourgeois and romantic relations. He paints a picture of each so that the reader can grasp the character of each as a whole. The bourgeois is painted in his home, the enlightened city, Paris. The depiction of Paris is outside the action of the novel, and, therefore, serves as a foil to the romantic relations in the novel. Paris is not alone in being a foil that is outside the action of the novel. The Upper Valais and Geneva play a similar role. These three societies clearly create a spectrum that outlines the human possibilities. The Upper Valais is a society dominated by nature; Paris is a society dominated by the arts and sciences; and, Geneva is a society dominated by civic virtue. Each of the ruling elements correspond to a kind of female beauty. Natural goodness, cosmopolitan charm, and conjugal virtue are the respective types. The three societies and their corresponding beauties are the key to figuring out Rousseau's literary opposition, as well as his departure from them. In *Pamela*, Richardson depicts both the simple goodness of a fifteen-year-old girl from a poor village, and her life as a virtuous wife and mother who is the mistress of an English country estate. In *Manon Lescaut*, Prévost depicts the sensuous charms of a young Parisian girl. The three societies and their corresponding females depict a spectrum of sexual relations that Rousseau rejects. The first chapter is devoted to the three societies and their female heroines.

While the first chapter is devoted to sexual relations that are dominated by the bourgeois, nature, and civic virtue, the second chapter discusses Rousseau's romantic reform of Christian piety, aristocratic honor, and patriarchal authority. This triumvirate also has its representative heroines, who, like Julie, are famous for their letters. Clarissa Harlowe is a Christian aristocrat whose virtue places her in opposition to her father's authority and the vindictive pride of both her brother and her suitor; and, Héloïse's love for Abelard places her in conflict with her vocation as a nun. Julie, however, is a lover, unlike Clarissa, and she is a mother, unlike Héloïse. Rousseau reforms the traditional authorities on the strengths of erotic and procreative attachments.

In the third chapter, I discuss love and family as romantic alternatives to the Enlightenment and Christianity. Love and family are actually syntheses of reason and belief. In attempting to harmonize religion and reason, Rousseau turns to classical philosophy. The ancient schools, unlike modern science, are not methods; they make claims about first principles, which give character to the life of reason. But, in using the ancient schools to bring harmony to reason and religion, Rousseau modifies classical philosophy by bringing the modern understanding of nature to bear upon the theoretical life. Rousseau completes reason through the love of a woman because he subjects the theoretical life to the body—to intercourse and to procreation. Julie is clearly a replacement for Socrates. Her death scene imitates the *Phaedo*; as Socrates finds himself surrounded by a Platonic lover (Kebes), an Epicurean beloved (Simmias), and a Stoic friend in need of support (Phaedo), Julie is married to an Epicurean, passionately loved by a Platonist, and admired by a Stoic. Rousseau's rhetoric is used to depict the apotheosis of a female, rather than a philosopher. Furthermore, by making Julie the centrepiece of *La Nouvelle Héloïse*, Rousseau also opposes pagan heroism. Julie replaces the fatherland as an object of honor and glory, just as she replaces God and knowledge. Rousseau is opposed to Plato and Plutarch, as well as Christianity.

Love and family are a mean between enlightened cosmopolitanism and Christian patriarchy. Yet, these two unities are not themselves united. They have two different and incommensurate ends, which bring them into conflict with one another. They give meaning to what are, in the beasts, inarticulate drives, but their reasons and pieties are not the same. The conflict between love and family gives romanticism its character. Its irresolvable conflicts make Julie's death a dramatic necessity. These conflicts can be seen in the character of Julie's renunciations and returns. The novel, as a whole, maintains the outline of biblical religion. Julie is a disobedient daughter who falls from virtue, only to return to God through marriage and family. But, upon her deathbed, she renounces her marriage and hopes to be reunited in heaven with her lover. Love and family belong together and apart because of the duality of man's sexual nature. Intercourse and procreation are inseparable, but distinct.

La Nouvelle Héloïse, taken as a whole, is an attempt to solve the conflict between nature and society by creating meaningful communities around intercourse and procreation. Nature, God, and reason are reformed to accord with love and family.

NOTES

1. Jean-Jacques Rousseau, *Second Discourse*, trans. Masters (New York, 1964), pp. 116–17.
2. Thomas Hobbes, *Leviathan*, ed. Macpherson (New York, 1981), ch. 11, p. 161.
3. Jean Jacques Rousseau, *The Reveries of the Solitary Walker*, trans. Butterworth (New York, 1982), ch. 5, pp. 62–73.
4. Jean-Jacques Rousseau, *Emile*, trans. Bloom (New York, 1978) p. 458.
5. Ibid., p. 357.
6. *Second Discourse*, pp. 213–20.
7. Ibid., p. 146.
8. Jean-Jacques Rousseau, *Letter to d'Alembert*, trans. Bloom (New York, 1960) pp. 83–89. In the pages cited above, Rousseau addresses himself to the feminists of his age. He does not mention them by name because he considers their arguments to be popular protests and prejudices, rather than thought.
9. Mary Wollstonecraft, *A Vindication of the Rights of Women* (England, 1992), p. 91.
10. *Emile*, p. 386.
11. *A Vindication of the Rights of Women*, p. 86.
12. Ibid., pp. 231–44.
13. *Emile*, p. 358.
14. Jean-Jacques Rousseau, *Julie ou La Nouvelle Héloïse* (Pléiade, 1964), II, xxi, p. 272. References are to part, letter, and page.
15. *Letter to d'Alembert*, p. 85.
16. Ibid., p. 83.
17. Ibid., p. 86.
18. Ibid., p. 134.

ONE

The Bourgeois, Nature, and Civic Virtue

Sexual Relations in Three Societies

Interpreters of *La Nouvelle Héloïse* have failed to understand love and family as possible solutions to the conflict between nature and society because they have failed to give adequate attention to the depictions of societies in the novel, which clearly create a spectrum. Paris, the Upper Valais, and Geneva are examples, respectively, of sophisticated cosmopolitanism, natural simplicity, and civic virtue. A recent translator has thought the discussion of these societies to be so far removed from the meaning of the novel that she has eliminated them entirely from her book.[1] By doing this, she has taken out a vital part of the novel. *La Nouvelle Héloïse* is not simply a romance, but is part of the history of political philosophy. St. Preux is interested in the best form of human association, and his travels help him investigate this question. *La Nouvelle Héloïse*, in this aspect, resembles *The Odyssey* and *Gulliver's Travels*, where travelling is accompanied by philosophic reflection on a variety of societies. In fact, *La Nouvelle Héloïse* closely resembles another novel that combined romance with travel—Prévost's *Le Philosophe Anglais ou Histoire de Monsieur Cleveland*. In that novel, there are adventures with a kind-hearted American tribe that has almost no art (certainly no science), a French commercial and cosmopolitan city, and a Protestant polis that is compared to Sparta. Furthermore, Prévost's novel also looks at love and family as associations that must be compared to the others, just as in *La Nouvelle Héloïse* love and family need to be understood in light of the problem and possibilities of Rousseau's spectrum. *La Nouvelle Héloïse* is

11

part of a distinguished tradition of philosophic-poetic texts, which teach by comparing and contrasting different societies.

La Nouvelle Héloïse is not, however, dominated by travel and adventure. Almost no action takes place in these societies to serve the main action, nor does anything happen in them to form a subplot. They are almost outside of the action and, therefore, give meaning to the novel by serving as foils which frame the entire work. They outline the human possibilities and, therefore, also correspond to the spectrum of subjects in Rousseau's major works. Paris is a cosmopolitan city where science and the arts claim to replace force and authority. It is the enlightened city and is the target of his criticism of the arts and sciences in the *First Discourse*. The people of the Upper Valais live in the remotest regions of the Alps. They have no commerce, poetry, or philosophy; they are described as a people almost out of the hands of nature. It is not difficult to see that their society is the closest one to nature in the novel, and that they accord most with *The Second Discourse*, where Rousseau takes man in search of his origins. Geneva is, of course, Rousseau's place of birth and the closest thing he found to the ancient city in modern times; it accords most with *The Social Contract*, which has political right as its subject.

The three societies are dominated by reason, nature, and civic virtue, respectively. But, they are not examples of nature, reason, and civic virtue, pure and simple. The Valaisian is not primitive man; the Parisian is not a philosopher; and the Genevan is not a classical citizen. In addition to not being pure, they are deficient because their mixtures lack harmony and scope. Love and family are possibilities which contain what is best about these societies, while avoiding what is worst in them. Natural goodness, truth and beauty, and the common good come together in love and family to form civilized relations superior to those in the other societies. By understanding the deficiency of these societies, we see love and family as solutions to their inadequacies.

PARIS

The section on Paris is by far the longest and the most important of the three. The Enlightenment was the dominant force of Rousseau's time, and he declared it victorious over throne and altar. In *The First Discourse*, we already have a general introduction to what is wrong with the enlightened city of Paris. Rousseau thought that Paris was the cosmopolitan city *par excellence*. All metropolises are inclined toward cosmopolitanism, but Paris was the first city to proclaim cosmopolitanism as a national philosophy and brought it as close as possible to its perfection. The *philosophes* were citizens of the world and, as Burke stated, they combined the ambition of politics with the atheism of Epicureanism. Rousseau was not a reactionary, and his thought played no small part in the overthrowing of throne and altar. He even affirms the truth of modern science and praises it for liberating man from a darkness worse than ignorance. But despite the liberation of the mind through science, there has been no progress in the more difficult task of self-knowledge—of knowing man's end and duties. Like a new Socrates, Rousseau calls man back from the ends of the universe to himself.[2]

Rousseau's objections to the cosmopolitan morality of Paris can be summed up in his simple observation that the European cosmopolitan loves the Turk half way around the world, so that he will not have to love his own neighbor at home. "Distrust the cosmopolitans who go to great lengths in their books to discover duties they do not deign to fulfill around them. A philosopher loves the Tartars so as to be spared having to love his own neighbors."[3] In other words, cosmopolitanism liberates man from the affections and duties to friends and family while connecting him to an abstract humanity for which he can have no genuine affection and for which he can perform no genuine deeds. By increasing man's attachments, cosmopolitanism weakens them. If there is less hatred, there is also less love. If there is more toleration, there is less belief in anything. Despite the goods provided by cosmopolitanism, and despite its overcoming certain prejudices, it only creates new and more destructive prejudices. It degrades the species. The species needs knowledge of its duties and ends, or self-knowledge, which is a form of probity or honesty. Neither science, nor cosmopolitanism, is capable of such virtue and awareness. Cosmopolitanism replaces virtue and inner awareness with politeness.[4] The city is proud of its politeness or what Rousseau also calls polish. It constitutes its good taste and education. The rusticity of the country and the virtues of a citizen would be offensive to polite society which requires the art of pleasantry or of offending no one, and here lies the rub. Politeness means falseness. Politeness means pretending to be concerned with others while thinking of oneself. These morals cannot but destroy the possibility of love and friendship, for there can be neither trust nor esteem among flatterers and pretenders. Politeness is suited for selfishness. It asks nothing in the way of a real sacrifice of interests, let alone of life, from its members and it even assists their interests since it liberates them from the demands of religion, politics, family, and even of romantic love. So long as one pretends to love everyone, one is free to love no one but oneself.

In addition to having no moral substance, politeness has no philosophic integrity. The rationality upon which cosmopolitans pride themselves is just a prejudice, or what is the same thing, the popularization of philosophy or pseudo-philosophy, which is a kind of ignorance. The fundamental cosmopolitan prejudice is that of reason itself. Had Voltaire been born during the time of the League, that is to say during times of religious fanaticism, he would have been a fanatic of a different stripe.[5] It has become too easy to be philosophic. A "dangerous Pyrrhonism" is the new prejudice; everyone is a relativist or what Rorty came to call an ironist. Reason is not a genuine insight, but a longing for permissiveness—to be free from religion, nation, and familial obligations, and ultimately to be free from reason itself which requires a self-explanation. Reason is not a freedom for anything and instead of culminating in free minds, promotes mass conformity to a herdlike existence. It is a kind of easy and smug nihilism. In the *Letter to d'Alembert*, Rousseau refers to Voltaire's play *Mahomet* as an instructive example. Voltaire presents Mahomet as a fraud and deceiver in order to liberate Muslims from their prophet, priests, and religious laws. In other words, Voltaire undertakes a Muslim enlightenment, but the attempt reveals Voltaire's own ignorance about both philosophy and religion. Religious fanaticism is not an error to be corrected through reason, but a blind zealotry. One can show followers that they are deceived but that will not make them any less fanatical. Rousseau says that one must leave the pen aside and pick up the sword.[6] Voltaire overestimated the power of reason because he did not want to believe in the necessity for war and ultimately only believed in reason as a means to polite society.

Cosmopolitanism replaces real philosophers with anthologizers or compilers who lack inspiration and whose task is to popularize philosophy, and thereby flatter the people by teaching them that all great things are for them and are accessible to them. In the ancient world, there was a sense of sacred mystery surrounding the highest knowledge. The gates of the Muses were closed to all but those who felt themselves strong enough to enter. Only men of the loftiest ambition and the greatest genius would dare to test themselves. Their reason, so far from being a prejudice, is exerted against religion, and develops itself by trying itself against its adversary. Reason does not languish in self-satisfied prejudice on account of its respectable conventionality. Furthermore, in addition to the absence of religious obstacles, there are no longer any political duties. As popularizers, the cosmopolitans have no contact with the responsibilities of political rule. Cicero, however, was consul of Rome and Bacon Lord Chancellor of England. Confronted with great responsibilities, their minds had a gravity and comprehensiveness lacking in the cosmopolitan, and they learned to reflect deeply upon philosophy and politics. Each of them undertook a kind of enlightenment for his nation. Cicero brought Greek philosophy to Rome and Bacon founded the modern scientific project in England.

The section on Paris in *Julie* is Rousseau's most extensive and thematic, and it throws new light on the victory of the Enlightenment by looking at its character independent of the antitheological ire, which heightened and lent legitimacy to its cause.

Rousseau introduces the section on Paris in a curious manner. He prefaces it with a footnote stating that, if he, himself, were to write the letters on it, he would write them differently than St. Preux.[7] He resisted, however, his temptation to alter the letters, because the reflections of a young man entering society for the first time should not be the same as those of an older man who has lived in it for many years. The footnote makes one think about how Rousseau would have differed in his account of Paris and whether he manages indirectly to communicate those differences. After all, would he arouse our curiosity if he did not intend to satisfy it?

The mere structure of the letters suggests that Rousseau's voice can also be heard.[8] They are remarkable in their organization by subject and by the subjects themselves. Each letter treats a fundamental part of human life. In the first letter, which has friendship and the common good as its subject, St. Preux discusses the civic relations between men. In the next letter, he discusses the things of amusement or taste, and it has as its subject poetry and philosophy. In the third letter, he discusses the relation between the sexes, and it has love and marriage as its subject.[9] In the final letter, he discusses music, and it has God as its subject. The letters are organized and comprehensive. And what is even more impressive about them is the diligence with which each letter probes the relation of the Parisians to each of these beings. If the Parisians are not citizens, philosophers, poets, lovers, husbands and wives, or devotees, then what are they? The answer is that they are nothing.

The Letters are a Comprehensive Account of Their Nonbeing

It is hard to believe that St. Preux is responsible for dividing up the letters in such a philosophic manner, since he writes them to satisfy the requests of Julie and Claire rather than according to his own plan. Furthermore, the tone of his letters and his actions in Paris bespeak youth rather than wisdom. He finds the Parisians to be both ridiculous and immoral, and undertakes the project to reform the morals of some military men who resent him and form a project to humiliate him and bring him over to their ways. He does not write like someone who has understood the character of Paris and who has resigned himself to its causes. His laughter, disgust, and hope is not quenched by his reason. There are two different sets of eyes brought upon Paris—those of a young lover and those of a philosopher.

St. Preux's letters are dominated by a tone of ridicule, not because he is a fop, but because he adopts the dominant tone of Parisian society in order to teach Julie about it and in order to relieve himself from its oppression. His letter on music (written at the request of the light-hearted Claire) is by far the funniest, since it ridicules what is dearest to the Parisians, most fanatically promoted and defended by them, and what is most credulous about them. The letter on the relations between the sexes (written to the more serious Julie) is the one letter on Paris whose tone is not predominantly one of ridicule. Those relations are so offensive to his sensibilities and pieties that he is amazed, indignant, disgusted, contemptuous, and full of pity. This lover cannot laugh when his god is insulted. The tragic response to Paris' sexual relations confirms his belief in his god, just as his laughter liberates him from their gods. But, for the most part, the section on Paris is a little comedy with two levels of laughter corresponding to the two different perspectives (there is even an underlying comedy in the letter on the sexual relations which corresponds to Rousseau's perspective). St. Preux's comedy is edifying. He ridicules the smallness of vice and the shallowness of vanity—two things that love elevates him far above. His tragedy is also edifying. It condemns hedonism and faithlessness between the sexes. Rousseau's comedy is much more philosophic; it requires reasoning about being, in order to evoke a smile. It is a comedy about a civilization that not only claims to be something, but to be everything, when, in fact, it is nothing. It is a comedy of being and nothingness.

The subject of comedy is something Rousseau has given serious consideration. In *The Letter to d'Alembert*, he takes issue with Molière.[10] He criticizes Molière for adopting the prejudices of polite society in order to succeed with it. Molière ridicules the authority and simplicity of fathers and celebrates the victory of sophisticated young lovers who have enlisted the help of the servants. Furthermore, not only does Molière ridicule fathers and the pieties connected with family, but he ridicules virtue itself. In *The Misanthrope*, he goes so far as to distort the character of real misanthropy in order to make virtue look ridiculous, but he never ridicules the fashionable or worldly man, because he is unwilling to show his audience to itself. Philinte emerges unscathed, while Alceste, the man of integrity, is made to fall in love with a coquette. Rousseau, on the other hand, like Montesquieu in *The Persian Letters* and like Muralt, himself, brings the eyes of an outsider to show Paris to itself. For all of Molière's genius and talent, he has neither an edifying surface, nor a philosophic core, because he adopted the prejudices of society as his model. The letters on Paris ridicule Molière's model.

St. Preux says that his criticisms of Paris are not personal, but are criticisms of large cities in general. Paris does not differ from London in any essential way. The only differences St. Preux finds worthy of note are that, in London, talent is more respected, and morals are slightly better.[11] This is attributed to the existence of a House of Commons. The people are part of the ruling public and, therefore, their character as a group influences the tone of society. Paris is part of St. Preux's investigation into the best form of human association, whether it is better to live crowded together in a city of six hundred thousand people or whether it is better to live in the remotest regions on the earth. Paris is not singled out from mean spiritedness or narrow provincial prejudices, but is representative of a place on the spectrum of human societies.

The first thing St. Preux feels in Paris is boredom and loneliness. These feelings are accompanied by a description: Paris is a chaos.[12] The city is busy and everything changes before one's eyes. Nothing can leave a lasting impression upon the senses and imagination, and therefore, on the heart. St. Preux is never more alone than when he is in society, and his only consolation is to lock himself up alone so that he can occupy himself with images and thoughts of his beloved. This first experience of Paris as an empty chaos where nothing can take hold of oneself is the decisive one. All that remains is to give an account of its lack of order and meaning.

St. Preux's first letter is about the civic relations between the men. He is struck by their friendliness and generosity. These are great civic virtues belonging to the ancient polis. St. Preux goes on to compare the Parisians with the Spartans. He says that the friendliness and generosity of the Parisians are false, that they are only a form of polite civility. Generous offers of wealth and assistance are so commonplace that those who make them do not even believe that they are taken seriously.[13] They trifle with the virtues of friendship because they have no respect for real friendship, and need a form of civility to replace real social feeling. St. Preux prefers Spartan frankness to false politeness.

> The honest interest in humanity, the simple and touching effusion of a frank soul have a language very different from the false demonstrations of politeness and the outward lies which the practice of the world requires.[14]

The genuine feeling of the Spartan is due to his being a citizen. He belongs to his country and is devoted to it. He has an awareness of the common good that makes his property, and even his life, less dear to him than his city and friends. St. Preux says that if the Parisians acted according to their speeches, then there would be perfect communism, since property seems to be the thing they value the least.[15] But, in fact, the discrepancy between rich and poor in Paris is greater than any place on earth.

The issue of property, which is inescapably connected to friendship and generosity, since friends are supposed to share everything in common, raises the question of the common good. The common good is, first and foremost, a political idea and leads to the question of the political thought of the Parisians. St. Preux says that politeness not only extends to sociality, but to political ideas as well. An idea or conversation is never pushed to the point of disagreement:

> Each states his opinion and supports it in a few words; no one attacks with zeal the one of the other; no one defends the opinion of his own.[16]

There is neither attack, nor defense, because there is indifference. The person stating his ideas does not even believe them; he certainly does not hope to persuade anyone of his thought. Ideas have the same falseness as generosity. This cynicism can be traced to the influence of party interest.

> It is not necessary to know the character of people, but only their interests, in order to divine nearly what they will say about each thing. When a man speaks, it is so to speak, his clothes and not himself.[17]

There cannot be any belief in justice when greed is so obtrusive and pervasive.

Yet, one might suggest that political life can be born from the interests of faction. What party cannot begin to believe its own ad hoc justifications when its interests are at stake? St. Preux goes on to show that the parties cannot even consistently pursue their interests. The two groups most worthy of note are the church and the military, which have God and country, respectively, as their cause. St. Preux says that priests put on the airs of a gallant, and artists that of royalty.[18] The lack of consistency between the outer appearance and the profession is due to a lack of inward cause. The military is no different. God and country are not simply reduced to interests because the force of factional interest is weakened by vain attempts to adopt the latest society fashions and to hold the latest opinions. The conflict between interests and vanity is the height of bourgeois absurdity. He cannot live for himself, nor for others. He is so incoherent that he cannot even pretend to have a reason for his life.

The absence of God and country raises the questions of who rules Paris and how it is ruled. A tyranny of physical force does not replace the lack of authority. On the contrary, the lack of authority has sapped the righteous anger which is an accompaniment of force. Yet, Paris is not anarchy either. It has rulers who despotically control the minds and actions of the entire city. After all, the church and the military are assimilated into a society. This society is not a political society since the authority and force it wields is not founded on justice and God, but is meant to replace them. In the second letter on Paris, St. Preux explains the peculiar character of Parisian despotism.

Paris is a gynaecocracy.[19] It is the women who rule. Not women in general, for then, their rule would be political; it would require a claim to justice in order to rule over men in general, and it would have to use force to defend that authority. It is the upper-class women who rule, and they rule in the only way they can—by making the male effeminate. Their rule is directed against force and authority, as force and authority would undermine their dominance. Because the women rule, their way of life dominates. St. Preux takes us into their lives in order to understand the character of their regime. St. Preux says that the love of amusement characterizes the women above all else.

> They seize things only by the pleasant aspect; all that ought to arouse anger and indignation is always badly received if it is not placed in a song or an epigram. The pretty women do not like to be angry, so

nothing angers them; and since there is no way to laugh at crime, the rogues are decent people like all the world. [20]

Their love of amusement is a love of laughter, and St. Preux goes on to say that it is ridicule that they love above all else. Ridicule replaces shame and force as instruments of rule. This tool makes them unjust and contemptible. They do not censure according to virtue and vice because they do not esteem virtue and cannot find vice in anything. They find ridiculous whatever does not conform to the manners of polite society and, therefore, will ruin a man who has lived a life of integrity if he should say the wrong word, while they will elevate a polished rogue. Besides punishing virtue and rewarding vice, they allow disorder by allowing crime to go unpunished. Anger is too disagreeable an emotion and punishment too harsh for their taste. In fact, a whole fiction about human beings and the world is fabricated to support their taste. Everyone in the world is decent, and, therefore, there is no need for force. They do not want to hear about murders and wars, and, thus, they do not exist or, at the very least, they are not necessary.

Since authority and force do not dominate, there is no rule of law. What replaces the rule of law are rules of propriety. The entire city slavishly follows general maxims of behavior and thought that have no basis in anything other than the decorum of the fashionable ladies. Real affection and thought are so truncated that there are even rules of propriety for love and mourning the dead. These fashions for good behavior and correct thought, which are enforced through slanderous ridicule, have no justification in reason, God, or nature, and do not express a felt need or sentiment. It is all opinion without reason or belief. It is a conformist society which has as its maxim of wisdom: "it is necessary to do like the others." [21]

This society that is opposed to force and authority, and which is dominated by the love of amusement, does, however, make some claims on its behalf. It claims to be enlightened. It boasts to have achieved the highest aspirations of philosophy and poetry by combining wisdom with amusement. Country and God are replaced by the salon and the theater. In and through these institutions, truth and beauty are supposed to find expression and justify humanity to itself.

St. Preux takes us into the salons and theaters in order to examine the relation of the arts and sciences to the lives of the Parisians. Morality and love are the great themes of their philosophic conversation, "a point of morality is not better discussed in a society of philosophers than at one of a pretty woman in Paris." [22] These conversations are not hypocritical justifications like the party platforms of the bourgeois, but they have a falseness of their own—that of high mindedness.

> [They] place virtue so high that even the wise cannot reach it . . . always philosophizing sadly, always degrading human nature through vanity,

always seeking in some vice the cause of what is done from goodness,
always after their own heart, meditating on the heart of man.[23]

Their moralisms are sombre and strict because they do not know of human goodness. They cannot imagine an agreeable disposition toward
helping other human beings. Furthermore, they can afford to be somber
and strict, because they have no intention of acting in accordance with
their speeches.

The cosmopolitan morality that comes to replace the morality of justice, goodness, and virtue is the morality of compassion. It does not require either authority or force, and it does not require real sacrifice either.
It is a moral sentiment as empty as their moral philosophy. It is a fleeting
feeling that does more to make one feel good about oneself than to relieve
the pain of the suffering. Once it is felt, its sweetness justifies one's humanity and makes one feel humane, even though one has not sacrificed
anything and even though suffering remains. There cannot be a real cosmopolitan morality because the tender feelings of pity are not enough to
inspire a sacrifice. For there to be a sacrifice of interest there must be an
understanding of the common good that overcomes the distinction between oneself and others. The abstract philosophy of morality and the
compassion without thought are two sides of the same coin. Neither can
bring about the necessary coherence between speech, feeling, and deed,
because there is no felt sociality that is buttressed by an idea of a common
good.

The morality of compassion is inextricably connected to the rule of
women. Force and authority—the arms of justice—necessarily undermine female rule because they are weaker than men. Compassion is an
attempt to replace justice by turning those with wealth and privilege into
beneficent mothers and fathers; it is an attempt by the upper-class wom-
en to justify to both the poor and to themselves, the enormous inequalities of wealth and privilege while denying the necessity for rule by force.

Rousseau is not a critic of compassion in general any more than he is a
critic of the influence of women in general. What he does object to is the
hypocritical use of compassion when it is pushed beyond the limits of
action and when the action depends on divine punishment and reward,
as is the case with Christian charity. Julie's compassion is never so general as to leave her impotent and, therefore, hypocritical and cold. The
heart cannot remain tender and sincere when the mind perceives the
impossibility of satisfying it. When Julie teaches St. Preux to put humanity before pleasure, she has him perform a good deed for an entrusted
neighbor. The limits placed on Julie's range of human relations allows
her compassion to be sincere.

The abstract character of their philosophy is even more recognizable
in their metaphysical discussions of love.[24] They do not know how to
speak its language because they do not know what it is. Love finds ex-

pression in poetry, not in general maxims. The enthusiasm for the true, the good, and the beautiful, without which love becomes a kind of commerce between the sexes, is foreign to their understanding and their way of speaking about it. Thus, their philosophic discussions of love, like those of morality, have nothing to do with their experience. What then is the philosophy upon which they pride themselves so much? It is yet another chapter on their vanity. St. Preux says that general maxims take the place of sentiment, because they are impressive; they have the appearance of comprehensiveness, and those that shout them out appear to be authorities speaking a rule of law. Furthermore, general maxims are directed toward agreement, rather than truth. They are not expressions of inner experience that need interpretation and justification. By virtue of being general, impressive, and directed at agreement, they have the character of law. But, the maxims make no claim to being authoritative. The impressive and the general produce agreement without either truth or obedience. It is simply a way of showing off to others and of filling a void by having everyone repeat and agree to the same thing, as if this agreement confirmed something real. Their abstract philosophy is neither reason nor belief; it is used to lend reality to nothing.

Having discussed the relation of philosophy to their lives, St. Preux goes on to discuss tragedy and comedy or the relation of art to their lives. The claim to instruct through amusement is Voltaire's public justification of the theater. St. Preux examines that claim. What is most striking about tragedy is that there is no attempt to maintain the tragic illusion.

> The actors, for their part, neglect entirely the illusion of which they see no one else cares. They place the heroes of antiquity between six rows of young Parisians; they trace the French fashion on the Roman dress. One sees Cornelia in tears with two fingers of rouge, Cato powdered in white, and Brutus in hose.[25]

There is no attempt to maintain the illusion, because no one expects the tragedy to seduce the audience. St. Preux contrasts this with the Greeks. The Greek tragedy has its source in politics.

> It offered to the Greeks an instructive and agreeable spectacle in the misery of their Persian enemies, in the crimes and follies of kings from whom the people were delivered.[26]

St. Preux emphasizes the historical and republican aspect of tragedy—the instructiveness and agreeableness of which cannot be experienced unless one has an understanding of what it means to defeat an enemy or dethrone a king. The theater can put Cato and Brutus in Parisian drag because the Romans mean nothing to an audience without political history and political life.

St. Preux also examines comedy in light of civic virtue. Comedy teaches virtue differently than does tragedy. While tragedy places on stage

characters and stories from the heroic past, comedy places on stage contemporary society. It seeks to educate toward virtue by showing its audience its vices. The contemporary comedy that St. Preux discusses cannot
show society its vices, because it cannot show society. Artisans and servants are not to be found on the stage, and from it, one would think that
to exist means to ride in a carriage and that those who walk are not
human. The comedy St. Preux discusses has moved further in the direction Molière took, for he was still able to show artisans and servants on
stage. The direction he took was one toward politeness rather than virtue,
and the comedy of St. Preux's time is the final act of polite society. The
marquesses have become so delicate that they cannot endure the sight of
people of low birth, and the comic genius has become so weak that the
authors try to make up for their inability to characterize by lending to
their comedies the attraction of famous names. Consequently, the stage
looks exactly like its audience and cannot, therefore, give them a perspective on themselves. Clever witticisms, little inside jokes, and embarrass-
ments dominate the comic stage. Their comedy hardly differs from their
dinner conversation where they ridicule their acquaintances.

While their tragedy fails the cause of civic virtue, because there is no
citizenry united by a heroic past, their comedy fails the cause of civic
virtue because it fails to ridicule the class differences which continually
threaten the common good. The upper and lower classes are brought
closer together when they can laugh together at one another and themselves. This is the way in which comedy helps to liberate men from convention, while strengthening their political union.

The Parisians have reversed the art of tragedy and comedy by destroying the dramatic illusion in tragedy and maintaining it in comedy.
By doing so, they destroy the belief in the subject of tragedy and political
virtue, while encouraging them to be earnest about the subject of comedy, themselves, and their paltry lives. Their lives not only dominate the
stage dramatically, but also in fact. The audience is literally on stage. The
upper class are the performers as well as the audience.[27] The spectators
care less about seeing the play than their friends on stage. The theater is
not a serious amusement, but a place where people go to see and be seen.

The theater is, then, not simply idle amusement, but is part of the
study of vanity—the bourgeois as actor and critic. Rousseau devotes a
footnote to this phenomenon where he compares the Parisians to the
Romans.[28] He retells a story about Laberius and Caesar. Caesar, piqued
by the noble liberty with which Laberius avenged his fading honor, punished him by forcing him on stage. No man of honor would be an actor,
because to be honorable means to be oneself, not to be so servile as to
speak and act differently from oneself for money and applause. When
Laberius went on stage, he gave a touching speech that was meant to
arouse pity for himself and indignation against Caesar. He spoke of having lived sixty years with honor, only to have lived a day too long. His

age is not ridiculed, but on the contrary, it arouses sympathy for his suffering. He juxtaposes his youthful strength with his infirm old age to both flatter the strong and to heighten the pity and anger of his audience. On another occasion, Rousseau refers to Lucrece as a female example of wronged and dishonored virtue, and he compares her effect in Rome with the effect she would have on the Parisians.[29] In Paris, her fate would only be met with laughter because they do not believe in the possibility of female chasteness and, consequently, ridicule, and despise those who boast of it. Likewise, Laberius' plea would only be met with the laughter of fops who despise the old and tolerate them, so long as they can laugh at them.

In the examples of Laberius and Lucrece, we see the rhetoric of trage-dy—suffering and dishonored virtue making itself loved and making vice odious and hated. The Parisian stage, on the other hand, is all talk and no action, just like their society. And the talk, with the exception of Racine, is shouted forth in general maxims like their philosophic lan-guage.[30] Their speeches are expressed in general maxims because there is no need for rhetoric. There is no need to persuade about the justice and honor of a cause, because interest and vanity are their primary causes. The audience would never be expected to take up arms against injustice and to give up their interests for honor. There is no art that can speak to their lives because they have no awareness of virtue. The respectability of actors reflects the emptiness of the audience. Public exhibitionism takes the place of virtue. Anyone who entertains gains applause, and anyone who gains applause is respected.

St. Preux's observations on the theater are not limited to reflections on virtue. He makes an interesting observation about how politeness affects death on the stage.

> If despair plunges a dagger in the heart, not content to observe the decency in falling, like Polixenes, he does not fall, decency keeps him upright after his death, and all those who have just expired return the instant after on their legs.[31]

Death is too ugly for the marquesses to look at. Like crime, there is no way to laugh at it, and, therefore, like crime, it is ignored. Decent society is to the women what money making is to the men—a way of avoiding confrontation with the eternal. The masking of death destroys the dra-matic illusion more than anything else and reveals why tragic art can have no relation to their lives. Their forgetting of death helps to explain why comedy is more akin to their lives than tragedy. But comedy is not a forgetting of death either. It temporarily liberates from its fears and ter-rors by creating a fantasy of impossible or, at least, unlikely circum-stances which keeps it away. The Parisian comedy is not a fantasy full of impossible or unlikely situations; it has little action and relies upon wit and lampooning. Their comedy is a vehicle for forgetting eternity. By placing themselves on stage and narcissisticly staring at themselves, they affirm to themselves that they are everything, and that theirs is the only possible world.

In reflecting upon St. Preux's letters on the theater, one sees that there is something missing from them. While he discusses the republican aspects of tragedy and comedy, he does not discuss love and religion. This absence is all the more striking considering the importance that Rousseau gives to these subjects in *The Letter to d'Alembert*. Furthermore, St. Preux refers to a love play, but he never treats it thematically. He mentions a play about a Roman emperor who chooses duty over love. St. Preux simply says that the subject (an emperor who knows duty and love) is so chimerical as to have no effect. The play, Racine's *Bérénice*, is treated extensively by Rousseau in *The Letter to d'Alembert*.

St. Preux's silence about the love interest in the theater is the only thing missing in his discussion of the relation between art and life in Paris. In the third letter, he discusses the Parisians' erotic lives, and, in the fourth letter, he discusses their piety and its artistic representation in music. The discussion of the artistic representation of love in *The Letter to d'Alembert* is a needed introduction to the third letter.

We should not be surprised that St. Preux does not discuss love and piety in the theater, because then he would have to reflect on the effects of love on family and country. No lover could think through these relations and still be a lover, for then he would have to turn love into a problem. St. Preux does not think that love is irreconcilable with familial piety and republican virtue. In the lover's mind, such conflicts are due to chance or prejudice, not necessity. Lovers do not believe that their love is a source of harm and conflict. St. Preux's silence about the love interest in the theater is a way of avoiding the problems of love.

In *The Letter to d'Alembert*, Rousseau writes as a citizen of Geneva, not as a lover. He can examine the influence of the love interest in the theater without compromising his love, which is that of his fatherland. The love interest belongs to a corrupt society.

> No longer able to maintain the strength of comic situations and character, the love interest has been reinforced. The same has been done in tragedy, to take the place of situations drawn from political concerns we no longer have, and of simple natural sentiments, which no longer move anyone.[32]

The sentimental and highly refined Racine gave prominence to love in his treatment of classical tragedy. The chimerical subject of a Roman emperor torn between duty and love (Antony was not an emperor) is flattering to the women of the French court. Just as Molière's comedy flattered the prejudices of his audience, the love tragedies flatter the power of the new rulers.

> Love is the realm of women. It is they who necessarily give the law in it, because, according to the order of nature, resistance belongs to them, and men can conquer this resistance only at the expense of their liberty. Hence, a natural effect of this sort of play is to extend the empire of the fair sex, to make women and girls preceptors of the public, and to give them the same power over the audience that they have over their lovers. . . . Look through most contemporary plays; it is always a woman who knows everything, who teaches everything to men.[33]

Rousseau's discussion of the love interest in drama is a continuation of the study of gynaecocracy.

There are those who defend the love interest in drama by arguing that in it men sacrifice love to duty, and women are punished for their weakness. *Bérénice* and *Zaïre* are the respective examples. At the beginning of *Bérénice*, the audience feels contempt for Titus, but at the end, after he has performed his duty, they cry for Bérénice and wish he had sacrificed his duty for her.

> In what state of mind does the viewer see this play begin? With a sense of contempt for an emperor and a Roman who sways, like the lowest of men, between his mistress and his duty. . . . What does the same spectator think after the performance. He ends up pitying this sensitive man whom he despised, by being concerned with the same passion which he considered criminal, by secretly grumbling at the sacrifice he is forced to make for the laws of his country.[34]

In *Zaïre*, we see the female audience seduced by love, despite seeing an innocent murdered by a jealous lover.

> When Orosmane sacrifices Zaïre to his jealousy, a sensible woman looks on the transports of passion without terror, for it is a lesser misfortune to perish by the hand of her lover than to be poorly loved by him.[35]

Both *Bérénice* and *Zaïre* teach that "the depictions of love make a greater impression than the maxims of wisdom, and that the total effect of a tragedy is entirely independent of the effect of the outcome. . . . If it [love] is well depicted, it overshadows everything that accompanies it. Its troubles, its sufferings make it still more touching than if it had no resistance to overcome."[36] Tragedy means that the ending is unhappy, but that there is justification and beauty in it; tragedy is necessarily pious and the tragedies of love teach belief in it. One thinks that suffering for love is a sacrifice to be esteemed and rewarded, and that it is pitiable because it is undeserving of suffering and suffers by chance, rather than by justice or by necessity.

The worship of this god is the only faith engendered by the theater. While classical tragedy is made into a matter of indifference by destroying the dramatic illusion, and comedy is made polite by keeping servants and tradesmen off the stage, love is idealized by presenting only prodigies of virtue in love.

> If a young man has seen the world only on stage, the first way to approach virtue, which presents itself to him, is to look for a mistress who will lead him there, hoping, of course, to find a Constance or a Cénie, at the very least . . . I know of no other play than the *Misanthrope* in which the hero made a bad choice. To make the misanthrope fall in love was nothing; the stroke of genius was to make him fall in love with a coquette. All the rest of the theatre is a treasury of perfect women. One would say that they have all taken refuge there.[37]

Rousseau argues that it is not the depiction of noble sacrifices to duty and the punishment of weakness that protects young men and women from this passion, but, rather, the depiction of error. He would rather see the stage full of fools and coquettes.

When the stage is full of perfect women, society is full of immodest ones. The Romans, on the other hand, depicted only slaves and prostitutes in love in the theater, and they had chaste ones at home.

> The ancients had, in general, a very great respect for women; but they showed this respect by refraining from exposing them to public judgement, and thought to honour their modesty by keeping quiet about their other virtues. . . . In a word, the image of open vice shocked them less than that of offended modesty. With us, on the contrary, the most esteemed woman is the one who has the greatest renown, about whom the most is said, who is the most often seen in society. . . .[38]

The dominance of the love interest in the theater is almost enough to prove that there are none worthy of it in society. Their love-dramas prove to be another example of art having nothing to do with their lives.

St. Preux's third letter examines the actual relation between the sexes. These relations occupy a middle ground between civic virtue and amusement. Love and marriage are forms of togetherness that require a common good and are accompanied by sweetness. The letter is also a continuation of the previous ones in so far as vanity emerges as the dominant social relation. In this case, it is a substitute for modesty, rather than civic virtue. The discussion of the sexual relations concentrate on the character of the women, just as the discussion of civic relations concentrated on the men.

St. Preux begins his discussion of the Parisian females with the surface—her appearance. It teaches him that they are more vain than modest. Their vanity is not, however, to be noticed in their rich adornments as one might expect. Their vanity reveals itself in their calculated immodesty, rather than their opulence. The marquesses, who set the tone for society, cannot compete with the daughters and wives of the merchants in terms of wealth, so they must find other ways of distinguishing themselves.

> It is, thus, that ceasing to be women, from fear of being confounded
> with other women, they prefer their rank to their sex, and imitate the
> girl of joy so as not to be imitated.[39]

Shocking immodesty is the surest way for a woman to separate herself from the pack.

The competition between riches and rank is not the only reason for the immodest appearance of the female. It is also a way for the ugly to distinguish themselves and even satisfy their hatred of the beautiful. By replacing the taste for the beautiful with the taste for the shocking, the ugly can shine, since ugliness shocks, while beauty is agreeable. The ugly not only avenge themselves on the beautiful by cultivating a taste for the disagreeable, but by getting the beautiful to make themselves ugly through fashionable clothes and behavior that is immodest. The ugly would rather be disgusting and cause indignation than be despised or ignored altogether. St. Preux advises them to be modest, because although ugliness is a barrier to passionate love, it is not a barrier to tenderness.

Although the replacement of modesty with immodesty begins with vain competition, it has far reaching effects, unintended by the initiators, which change the relation between the sexes and the entire tone of society. Shocking immodesty changes the nature of female pride. It teaches that the most honorable woman is the one who is desired the most, which means by the most men. She is necessarily a coquette, promising to do everything for every man. Sex and vain attentions make up her erotic life. Modesty, on the other hand, cannot be reduced to either passion or opinion. While it is true that it accompanies an awareness of sexual desire and a fear for one's welfare and reputation, it cannot be reduced to these elements because it is informed by love. It is accompanied by a desire for an exclusive and permanent attachment. Modesty is a virtue that proves a woman's worthiness and respect for it proves a man's.

The immodesty of the female is an open declaration of her sexual desire. This openness poses problems for defense. The malicious ridicule that dominates society has its source in her attempt to disarm those who would scorn her, and/or make advances. This combination of sex and ridicule constitutes the female regime and is characterized by negativity, because it is deficient in love. Her sexuality has no articulate end other than the animal act and cannot, therefore, be the basis of a social order containing shame and esteem. Her regime is necessarily shameless and defensive. It is not informed by any inner conviction about her beauty and goodness. The use of ridicule is an attempt to defend the indefensible. The dominant tone of Paris is one of defensive and joyful negativity, and it is inescapably connected to the character of its rulers.

What little dramatic action that does take place in St. Preux's letters on Paris helps the reader to understand female ridicule.[40] St. Preux goes to Paris not only as an observer, but as a lover. He must survive the temptations of the city as well as those of himself. Julie is worried that he will corrupt his attachment to her through habits of imagination and opinion. He does, in fact, take a fall, but he commits a crime against love for which he can repent. He does not contract a habit of the imagination and of the mind, which would corrupt him beyond return. St. Preux is unknowingly taken to a brothel where he is slipped some wine and awakens in the arms of a prostitute. On his way out the door, he hears the prostitutes laughing at him as they hang out the window. Their ridicule is vindictive as well as a force used to make him conform to their ways. Ridicule is anger and shame without righteousness. It does not persuade the heart or the mind, because it makes no claim to the true, the good, or the beautiful. St. Preux's love triumphs over the forces of Paris. It is true that, when he does discover he is in a whorehouse, he stays there from fear of ridicule, but his shame avenges outraged love. He confesses his crime to his goddess rather than try to deceive her. He never excuses his crime and he never becomes an accomplice of those who try to corrupt him.

St. Preux is never morally outraged at prostitutes, though he finds them odious. Like the Romans, he is less shocked by open vice than offended modesty. Prostitutes are beneath his indignation because they could never be an object of his affection, nor insult an object of his affection. Prostitutes are not objects of Rousseau's indignation either. There is a subplot in La Nouvelle Héloïse concerning prostitution. Fanchon is a poor neighbor of Julie who is driven to desperation by her poverty. A wealthy man from the city offers to take care of her and her infirm father if she becomes his mistress. Julie uses her charity to save her from this fate and to have her married by arranging to have her suitor released from his obligations to the military. Joining a prince's militia is the male version of prostitution in the novel. This story is taken from Prévost's Man of Honour and can be understood only when compared to it.[41] Prévost's hero gives money to a prostitute who has told him that she is new to the trade and entered it out of desperation rather than disposition. She takes his money promising to leave the trade and take up a decent occupation. He later discovers that everything she said was a lie and that she only thought of taking advantage of his attraction and pity. In the city, generosity and goodness are stifled by distrust. The development of their minds has given them the sophistication to lie to one another. This distrust has everything to do with the influence of money. It buys what is supposed to be shared by tender hearts. Its purchasing power makes it an arbiter of all human relations and thereby destroys virtue and love.

The prostitutes and the marquesses have a great deal in common and are clearly meant to be compared. St. Preux goes to both for a dinner party and he discovers that both share a taste for immodesty and ridicule. The negativity or indifference to the true, the good, and the beautiful, which characterizes both of these groups, is a reaction to wealth's arbitration of affection and honor. The prostitutes and marquesses are partners in a reactionary anticommercial culture. The prostitutes try to corrupt modesty with ridicule and sex in order to reduce everything to their level, while the marquesses try to shock modesty with ridicule and sex in order to distinguish themselves. The poetry and philosophy on which they pride themselves has nothing to do with their souls. It is a pretence to sophistication without which they would appear to be no different than the prostitutes. Ridicule is the tool of vice, whereas righteous indignation is the sword of virtue. The misanthrope is angry at his fellow men because he expects them to be virtuous. He thinks they are responsible for themselves, and he loves them enough to be angry at them. Ridicule, as a dominant social force, has as its goal the corruption and impotency of virtue. The alliance of the prostitutes and the marquesses is the fruit of Molière's comedy. The cultivation of the arts and philosophy only leads to a critical and philistine culture. Slanderous ridicule, opportunism, and exhibitionism masquerading as free thinking and artistic criticism are the fruit of Molière's comedy and the Parisian gynaecocracy.

St. Preux does more than explain the sexual politics of Paris. He also shows us the erotic lives of the marquesses. Their marriages and loves are not very different from those of prostitutes and their clients. What is most striking about their erotic relations is the easy familiarity between the sexes. He contrasts this easy familiarity with the example of the Swiss:

> Our Swiss women love to assemble themselves together; they live there in sweet familiarity, and, although it appears that they do not hate the appearance of men, it is certain that the presence of them throws a sort of constraint on their little gynaecocracy.[42]

The opposite is the case with the Parisian ladies. A woman is comfortable in an apartment full of men, and only becomes disconcerted when another woman enters. In fact, they cannot even put their dislike for one another aside to go to the theater, which they love and where custom requires that they be accompanied by another woman. A vain woman prides herself on the attentions of men and is constrained by the competition from other women as well as their judgment. Modest women, on the other hand, enjoy one another's company and can even be friends because they share a concern with the virtue and reputation of their sex. Their modesty makes easy familiarity between the sexes impossible because it accompanies an awareness of sexual differences and the serious character of the union between the male and the female. Easy familiarity between the sexes presupposes a lack of gravity between them.

The easy familiarity between the sexes requires a male character as well as a female. While the female is a coquette, the male is a gallant. His gallantry is an empty form. He knows what he wants and how to win it. He gives attentions in order to receive favors. It is true that St. Preux longs to be rewarded, and that Julie enjoys his praises of her, but St. Preux's sexuality and Julie's amour-propre are connected to ideas about truth, goodness, and beauty. They have inner sentiments and ideas about the meaning of their connection. The coquette and the gallant lack all of this; they are debased lovers.

St. Preux says that there have been apologists for the free relations between the sexes who argued that "by multiplying temptations, one would conquer them."[43] But, all the world now agrees that affairs are the fruits of the commerce between the sexes. Permissiveness leads to the most intolerable abuses, which not only cause general disorder, but destroy the soul. He traces for us the fates of the coquette and the gallant. He begins his discussion of their story with their marriage:

> It seems only to be an agreement between two free persons who agree to live together, to have the same name, to recognize the same children; but who have, besides, no sort of right on one another.[44]

Fidelity is not part of marriage. The male who attempts to keep his wife honest would appear in public as ridiculous as the wife who is honest. There is neither an authority to keep them loyal, nor is there a felt sentiment accompanying a moral understanding because "whoever marries only for fortune or status owes nothing to the person."[45] St. Preux is indignant and horrified by the spectacle of permissiveness. He is angry that "women who do not fear to soil one hundred times the conjugal bed would dare from an impure mouth to accuse [his] chaste love and condemn the union of two sincere hearts, who are sure never to lack faith."[46] The consequences, with respect to faithlessness, disturb him even more. The idea of a father tenderly hugging his child, while doubting whether it is his own, is one that tears at his heart.

St. Preux is also disturbed, in the sense of being dumbfounded and chilled, by the indifference lovers feel for one another:

> Lovers are indifferent persons, who see another because of amusement, looks, habit, or the need of the moment. The heart has nothing to do with these connections; one only consults convenience and certain agreeable, exterior features.[47]

They are so indifferent to one another that lasting recognition is not even a consequence of their encounters:

> If the fantasy should take to renew [their love], they would have a new acquaintance to make, and it would be much for them to remember having seen one another.[48]

Their concern with one another is momentary. The attentions sought by the coquette do not amount to anything. She cares about the opinions of a man who will be faceless to her shortly afterward. There is nothing substantial about her sense of self. Furthermore, the favors, which the gallant enjoys, are nothing or, at least, not what he thinks them to be. He has a sense of self as a consequence of being chosen, but any man would have served the purpose. In these relations, we see false attachments, like the ones of the bourgeois, except that it is not interest which is the truly felt need, but the desire for intercourse. And, like the bourgeois, the lovers belong to neither themselves, nor to each other. They cannot simply satisfy their desires without the concern for opinion because they must have it to get what they desire, and they cannot consider themselves attached to their partner in any meaningful way.

St. Preux says that sometimes the women take to the whimsy of taking their husbands as lovers, because, after all, they, too, are men. The relations between men and women are homogenized by sexual desire to the extent that faith and betrayal become meaningless. But, the relation is never simply animal because of the influence of amour-propre. The false respects between the coquette and the gallant are not, however, the final act of their sexual play; they conclude with mutual contempt. The gallant is too familiar with what is offered and to how many to be impressed with it, and the coquette is too familiar with routine attentions to be flattered. They learn to despise the sexuality of one another because the bad faith is so obvious that they cannot even pretend to believe the illusions that save the pretense to respect and integrity. Yet, oddly enough, this cynicism leads to a new kind of attraction. Contempt for women becomes admired.

> It is no less essential to French gallantry to despise the women as to serve them. This contempt is a sort of title, which is conferred by them; it is a witness that one has lived enough with them to know them.[49]

The sexual relation is turned on its head. Modesty taught women to respect men who respected them because they thought themselves worthy of respect. Their admiration for the male who knows enough to despise them proves that they despise themselves. Chastity, in fleeing the female, becomes the virtue of the male. The female must now submissively seek to be degraded, rather than saucily flaunt herself.[50]

These sadomasochistic relations, however, make as little sense as the relations founded on coquetry and gallantry. If the male were truly contemptuous of the female, he would not have sex with her, not even to display his disdain. And if the female were truly impressed by the contempt of the male, she would not offer herself, even for the purposes of punishment and humiliation. They are no more successful at being completely apart than they are at being together. It is no wonder that they speak of love in general and metaphysical terms. Their abstract language, which means nothing to them, is used to describe nothing. These abstractions help them avoid the nothingness of their private relations by giving a pretence to explanation and by having others agree to it. *La Nouvelle Héloïse*, on the other hand, is nothing but the attempt to find legitimate expression of sexual desire. St. Preux's description of the relations between the sexes is, therefore, not only one of amazement, disgust, indignation, and pity, but also of incoherence. Their amour-propre conflicts with their sexual desire, just as it conflicts with their interests.

The sexual relations of the Parisians strike at the heart of religion. The gods live and die by respect for ancestral authority. The indifference of the Parisians to the sacredness of marriage makes one wonder if piety has any place in their lives. In the fourth letter on the opera, St. Preux shows us in what they believe. Their opera is their religion. They are not passionate about country, God, love, or family. St. Preux can speak about these things openly with them, but foreigners do not dare speak their minds about the opera:

> It is not as free as you think it, to speak your opinion on this subject. Here, one can dispute everything except their music and opera.[51]

While virtue is ridiculed and vice goes unpunished, they unleash their righteous indignation in defense of their music.

What is even more indicative of their belief in the truth, beauty, and goodness of their opera is that they are seduced by the stage props, even though they are clearly and painfully artificial. St. Preux is bored by the opera precisely because he cannot believe in the stage illusions. The lack of reality disengages his heart and imagination from the entire production. He looks at it in a comic vein because it takes seriously what does not exist. He laughs at their piety, writing paragraphs on the ridiculous appearance of what seduces them. The fourth letter is a work of blasphemy, and in order to understand it, one must understand the god he insults.

The opera is the closest thing to the religious tragedies of the Greeks. It combines drama with music, song, and dance. Music, song, and dance are the sensual accompaniments of belief. They persuade and confirm through the assurance of rhythms and movement where reason falls silent. While the Parisians cannot take seriously classical tragedy, they can be enthusiastic about the subject of their operas. The subject is the divine in its most marvellous manifestations. The pagan gods, the chariot of the sun, the heavens, the seas, monsters, and devils are all found there. It is an ecumenical stage belonging to no tradition and embodying no particular duties. So long as it dazzles, it has a place on stage. All of this is more believable to them than the possibility of Cato's existence because they judge Cato to be a man and find him too different from themselves to allow him reality. The gods, on the other hand, being different from them can be anything and be believed. They are credulous concerning the fantastic and dubious about virtue and goodness.

Their music and song reflect their taste for the marvellous. The singers shout and contort their bodies such that one is not sure which is more offended, the eyes or the ears. They try to sound and look as big as the props. The music is as much a failure as the song in its attempt to be big. St. Preux says that the audience begins to tap their feet if the music happens upon something with rhythm. He says that the Italians never tap their feet because their music engages their souls. The Parisians tap their feet to rhythm because it is a relief from boredom. Their music does not touch them; it is pretentious and bloated.

Nor does their dance touch them. Dance does not imitate anything and must, therefore, be an accompaniment to music. But the dance takes place during the intermission as a kind of entertainment that has no relation to the drama and its music. There is no unity to the arts. The opera, like their society and their souls, is a boring chaos. The chaotic and uninteresting character of the opera is further evidenced by the sight of the actors sitting on the stage during the intermission. They do not even try to maintain the dramatic illusion because the audience is not gripped by the drama. Neither the music nor the story captures the imagination of the audience.

What, then, is the piety inspired by the opera? St. Preux answers the question at the end of the letter. He says that unless he had seen it, he would not believe there to be artists so feeble as to represent on stage what should only be imagined and an audience so childish as to go see it. The piety of the Parisians is the piety of a child, and there lies the key to understanding them. The taste for the marvellous produces a momentary sense of awe and is then soon forgotten. It is simply a flash with no connection to love or duty, because, like children, they are incapable of sentiment.

Why, then, do they angrily defend it if it has no relation to their lives? The answer lies in amour-propre. The opera fills them with feelings of depth and importance. It is bombastic. The ridiculous belief in the stage props mirrors the ridiculous belief in themselves. The opera tries to look and sound gigantic in order to flatter the audience's sense of self. They are the object of their piety. In defending the opera they defend their own sense of importance.

In the earlier letters it was shown that justice and love were not taken seriously by Parisians as objects of truth because they lack both a public-spirited concern for the common good and the faith required for love. Belief and indignation do not belong to their erotic and political lives because there is not even an illusion of truth. One cannot believe in and become indignant about one's interests and sexual passions if one thinks that they are simply one's selfish desires. Even the belief and indignation accompanying the opera have a tenuous character. They are accompanied by a sense of self-importance, but the self is inarticulate. The music fills them full of themselves, but does not give them any reason to think that they are anything. Without an attachment to country, God, family, or love, they fall back on themselves as a source of pride, but they have nothing to be proud of. Their piety and indignation do not, therefore, accompany a self-understanding that can overcome the shameless negativity that is the tone of the society as a whole. St. Preux, therefore, ends his discussion of Paris by saying that they deserve the bad, not because they do not know the good, but because "the pleasure of the critic consoles them for the boredom of the spectacle, and it is more agreeable to mock it when they are no longer there, than to enjoy themselves when they are there."[52] He ends his discussion with reference to their childish and malicious laughter.

The letters on Paris are a comprehensive criticism of cosmopolitanism, which have a single thread running throughout them that the Parisians lack the coherence for meaning and are, therefore, without character or self-articulation. This failure of civil man to attach himself to others is inextricably connected to his failure to situate himself in relation to eternity. In the section on taste in *Emile*, Rousseau criticizes the moderns and shows that death is the issue. He writes,

> No one could make an agreeable lot for himself if he were constantly living in contradiction with himself. It is, thus, that Empedocles reproached the Agrigentines for cramming in pleasures as though they had only a day to live, and building as though they were never going to die.[53]

This criticism is directed at the Parisians, who are being used as an example of the modern failings. Their lives are incoherent because their ambitions conflict with their pleasures. This conflict is traced to their failure to bring their ambition and pleasures under the tutelage of an idea of death and eternity. At one moment they grab for pleasures as if they were about to die, and, at another, they accumulate as if they had forever to put aside for their pleasures. Their vacillation is a way of avoiding death in the pleasure of the moment, or, the business and vanity of ambitions.

Rousseau gives us an example of some epitaphs to show the bad taste of the moderns and the good taste of the ancients, all of which relate to death. He gives four examples:

> Stop, passer-by; you are trampling on a hero.
> I built Tarsus and Anchialus in a day, and now I am dead.
> They died irreproachable in war and friendship.
> Passer-by, tell them in Sparta that we died here to obey her holy laws.[54]

The first is typical of the moderns and the last three of the ancients. The modern tombstones are filled with praise, while the ancients, with facts. The first epitaph has the bombastic character of a man who wants to be thought of as a god. The second shows the humility of a man reduced to nothing. The last two show men sacrificing themselves. Modern man has no duties to perform and is too vain to think that he will be reduced to nothing. The bombast characteristic of their tombstones, their music, and their philosophy is a consequence of not living in relation to death, for only a man who has forgotten death would try to bloat himself into a god.

In another passage in *Emile*, Rousseau states most clearly the necessity for habits of continuity, for images and opinions about the permanent, in order to make man truly social.

> I would even want the pupil and the governor to regard themselves as so inseparable that the lot of each in life is always a common object for them. As soon as they envisage from afar their separation, as soon as they foresee the moment which is going to make them strangers to one another, they are already strangers. Each sets up his own little, separate system; and both, engrossed by the time they will no longer spend together, stay only reluctantly.[55]

The belief in shared fates is completely absent in Paris because there is nothing beyond themselves. Poetry, philosophy, and music have no genuine connection to their lives because they do not have a world in which to live. They do not even have a semblance of being, and thus cannot have an articulation of themselves or of the world. Their expressions consist of slander, frivolity, bombast, abstract maxims, and sophistic defenses of their interests and their vices because they have no inner awareness of themselves, their relation to others, and their relation to eternity. This is Rousseau's anatomy of modern man, the anatomy of the citizen of the world who thinks he is everything when in fact he is nothing.

THE UPPER VALAIS

The Upper Valais and Geneva are much more to St. Preux's and Rousseau's taste than is enlightened Paris, but they are also deficient. The people of the Upper Valais are almost fresh out of the hands of nature.[56] They are a mountain people, with almost no connection to the rest of the world. Their isolation is accompanied by a disinterested love of humanity. Unlike the Parisians, they are hospitable and would not think of taking a penny from St. Preux. Generosity is a virtue belonging to them rather than the Parisians, because they know that those who visit them are not doing so for money, but from love. Furthermore, there is no conflict between their interest and giving because they receive so few visitors. They are poor, but can afford to be generous because of limited demand. They also differ from the Parisians in that they do not attempt to force St. Preux to live according to their manners; he is given total freedom to live as he is accustomed. He has this freedom because they themselves follow the promptings of nature more than law or opinion. St. Preux makes no mention of any political parties and religious sects. The domestic men sit at the table with their masters and sons become the equals of their fathers upon reaching the age of reason. Their lives reflect the simplicity of nature.

The Upper Valais is an example of a rustic republic. There is great respect for old age and the men are the heads of the household, but this is due less to authority than to a division of labor rooted in the differences between the male and female body. The men labor for sustenance, and the women look after the house and children. There is not enough wealth to free them from necessity. But it is precisely in living according to necessity that they have their charm. They are free from the criminal, petty, and perverse that dominates Paris. They could not even imagine what is a matter of course for Parisians; they have the charm of innocence. It is doubtful whether they could imagine intercourse independent of procreation. Their imaginations are surrounded by nature and they themselves come into being and go out of being almost like the seasons — without fear, piety, and ceremony. This naturalness is found in their young maidens. They will blush if a man should only look at them. This is in stark contrast to the shameless blush of the Parisian women who use artifice (rouge) in order to distinguish themselves and attract a male.

Yet, there are also disagreeable aspects to the people of the Upper Valais. Their ugliness is most noticeable at the dinner table. Throughout *La Nouvelle Héloïse*, there are many scenes around the dinner table. There are the dinners in Paris, the dinner at Vevey, the dinner at Clarens, and the dinner with the Valaisans. Rousseau sees in these dinners a snapshot of their societies; they are little symposiums. A dinner requires that a small group of friends come together at a moment of leisure. It is a time when the needs of the body are being met, but when the acquisition and competition for goods is forgotten. The mind and imagination can free itself, if only momentarily, from the concern for the body, because everything is secure before it. This moment is, therefore, a window in which one can see human beings together and undivided by competition.

The ugliness of the Valaisans at the dinner table is due to their lack of philosophy and poetry. They have goodness, but not truth and beauty. They do not live with an eye toward leisure, but toward work. They are simple and rustic, but also coarse. Their coarseness, however, does not partake of the sensual as does the Parisian. But, it shows a lack of tenderness and virtue. Their young girls stand behind the chairs of the old men at the dinner table because their charms are subordinate to respect for old age. Even the women of the magistrate are treated like servants. And the women, like the men, are also lacking a love of the true and the beautiful. The ease with which they blush, although preferable to immodesty, reveals a lack of sentiment and virtue. They would blush less often and less easily if they had more discernment between men and were more serious about their relations with them. Love does not belong to them because the force and image of nature determines the relations between the sexes.

The men are especially disgusting at dinner because they drink until they are drunk. They have not developed their minds enough to enjoy conversation; they have little politics, religion, or love, because they have no experience of beauty, and, hence, no need to articulate it. The limitedness of their minds is certainly to be preferred to the development of the

Parisian mind, which is used for lying to one another and oneself, but it makes them unfit for leisure. St. Preux and Rousseau prefer the rustic aristocracy to the rustic republic.

GENEVA

The Genevans, on the other hand, are well read and converse a great deal. But this does not necessarily bode well for love and family. Claire's father, who is very politically minded, ignores her altogether in order to read the paper and discuss the issues of the day. It is appropriate that Claire discuss Geneva, because romance has little place there. Furthermore, she has little interest in politics (even despises it), and by having her make the commentary, Rousseau avoids a discussion of politics, which does not belong in a romantic novel. La Nouvelle Héloïse is about the domain of Julie, and as St. Preux's account of Paris makes clear, her domain is not politics.

Although the Genevans are the closest thing to Sparta in the modern age, they are still very far from it. Despite their sumptuary laws, they are very commercial, and those who bring back fortunes from foreign business ventures are well received. They are, in fact, closer to England than they are to Sparta, and Rousseau says that the sexes live separately in the English manner.[57] Claire's letter discusses almost exclusively the character of the women and can be considered a commentary on the romantic limits of Protestant commercial republics.

What is most remarkable about the girls Claire overhears is that they sound much older than they are. They are lively and chaste but they speak with a clarity and directness that is uncharacteristic of young teens. The influence of civic life has left its imprint on the women; they are too imbued with that aspect of citizenship that requires clear thoughts and communication to be subject to the mad passion of love. In fact, Rousseau even objects to the excessive separateness between husband and wife. Wolmar makes his household his life; he does not engross himself in politics.

LITERARY REPRESENTATIONS OF
SEXUAL RELATIONS IN THE THREE SOCIETIES

In creating a frame of problems and possibilities for La Nouvelle Héloïse, Rousseau not only had before his mind Paris, the Upper Valais, and Geneva, he also had literary works in front of him, which showed the kind of sexual relations dominated by these associations. La Nouvelle Héloïse is not only a combination and refinement of these associations, but of his great literary predecessors as well.

La Nouvelle Héloïse is the greatest literary success known. Its impact was immediate and far reaching, making the novel the dominant literary form, even to this day. Its success has prompted studies in the history of the novel, and the novelistic influences on *La Nouvelle Héloïse* have been studiously explored. Daniel Mornet's introduction to his edition of *La Nouvelle Héloïse* is the most famous, and has made him a source of enlightenment on the subject. But, Mornet's discussion of Rousseau and his literary predecessors suffers from a lack of order. He gives us a long list of all the novels written before Rousseau, and when he does undertake comparisons, they are brief and undeveloped. One does not get the sense that Rousseau is actually engaged in a debate with these authors, but rather, that something of them rubbed off on him. This presentation of the relation between Rousseau and his literary predecessors is too loose. Rousseau borrows the forms, names, and plots of authors, not because he is unimaginative, or, because they have rubbed off on him from contact, but because he wants to point to his opposition and show the reader where he disagrees with the other alternatives.

Rousseau's works imitate in order to separate and clarify his own thought. The *Second Discourse*, his book on man's origins, is an imitation of Genesis and Book V of Lucretius' *On Nature*; and it also takes aim at the state of nature theories of Hobbes and of Locke, not to mention Aristotle's understanding of nature. *Emile*, his book on education, is an imitation of Plato's *Republic*. His *Confessions*, the book about his own education, is an imitation of St. Augustine's *Confessions*. *The Social Contract*, which has the principles of political right as its subject, is an imitation of Locke's *Two Treatises on Government*. And *La Nouvelle Héloïse* is an imitation of the novels of Prévost and Richardson. He points to them in form and substance. *La Nouvelle Héloïse* is a novel of letters with twelve engravings divided into two parts—a perfect imitation of *Pamela*. Like *Pamela* and *Clarissa*, there are two titles, the first of which is the name of the female protagonist. As for substance, I have already mentioned the remarkable extent to which it imitates Prévost's *Cleveland*. Prévost and Richardson are Rousseau's admired literary opponents. There is no need to look beyond them, leafing through dozens of other novelists, until one has sifted all one can from these sources.

As has already been indicated, *La Nouvelle Héloïse* is a novel that distinguishes the different character of sexual relations in different societies. The sexual differences between Paris, the Upper Valais, and Geneva are reflected in *Manon Lescaut*, the first part of *Pamela*, and the second part of *Pamela*, respectively. These portray defective relations between the sexes consistent with the defects of the three societies.

Manon Lescaut is a love story that takes place in Paris. The love between Manon and Grieux is dominated by sensuality. He finds her charms, rather than her goodness and virtue, to be her greatest attraction. St. Preux's name is an imitation of Des Grieux, and much can be learned from their different meanings. The name of Prévost's heroic lover is derived from the word for grief, whereas St. Preux's name is derived from the word for worthiness. Prévost chose the name because he wanted to warn young people about the dangers of love. He says that his novel is "a moral treatise entertainingly put into practice."[58] It is meant to teach that friendship, consisting of shared conversation about morals, makes up the most agreeable part of life. But, as we have learned from the *Letter to d'Alembert*, its effect is quite to the contrary, because the total effect is independent of the final conclusion. Prévost's novel teaches the opposite of what he claims in the preface. Des Grieux is by far the most impressive character in the novel, and his sufferings make us sympathetic to his love. At the end of the novel, he returns to his friend Tiberge, whom he abused and who remained constant to him despite it. But, Tiberge does not win our sympathy. Love triumphs over everything in the novel despite its crimes and sufferings.

Manon is a coquette. Grieux is continually torn between his love for her and his distrust for her, even disgust and disdain for her. Prévost does not paint her as malicious, or even capricious, but as corrupted by a love of amusement and luxury. She will compromise on fidelity, unaware that she is insulting love, in order to have the money for entertainments and trinkets. Her need for money drives Grieux into a life of crime that moves from disobedience and lying, to theft and murder. Her taste is, therefore, responsible for corrupting his morals; their love does not accompany goodness and esteem for virtue.

By naming his lover St. Preux, Rousseau draws attention to the different character of his love story. St. Preux must be worthy of his beloved because she is virtuous and good, as well as charming. Unlike Prévost, Rousseau attributes to love an element of the divine. St. Preux must sacrifice his pleasures and his happiness in order to prove himself worthy of his goddess. As is evident from Rousseau's comments on the total effect of love tragedies (in the *Letter to d'Alembert*), he gave considerable thought to the end of his novel. Rousseau's novel is dominated by romantic love, a longing for a return to a lost happiness which one has sacrificed in order to be worthy of it. Prévost's novel, on the other hand, is more pathetic than romantic. Manon does eventually give up entertainments and luxury, and is faithful to Grieux, but it is a love dominated by pity rather than esteem and goodness. She is exiled to America, and it is upon that exile, when she has lost hope for an easy and amusing life, that she looks at Grieux with a pitiful eye and realizes that she has treated him poorly, not unworthily. She does not esteem herself enough to esteem him and, thus, returns to humanity by way of pity and guilt. Their love ends with a pathetic scene of death, untempered by hope and admiration; Grieux's love ends with inconsolable grief. It is a love without hope that haunts his memory and brings sweet tears to his eyes, but which has no world to support it. He renounces it while savoring it; he does not return to virtue with his heart. Prévost, far from leading men to virtue by show-ing the grief of a lover, has only made virtue look unattractive as a harsh return to reality.

As *Manon Lescaut* is a story of the city dominated by Manon's charms, *Pamela* is the story of a girl from a poor rustic village, whose simple goodness reforms the morals of an aristocrat, and even overcomes his prejudices. The first part of *Pamela* is about her life as a daughter and humble servant. The second part is about her life as a wife and mother, who is the mistress of a country estate. *Pamela* is not a love story. There is a courtship, of a sort, in the first part, but there is too much force, decep-tion, and bribery involved to call it romantic. The advances made upon her are an insult to humanity and familial piety as well as female virtue. Her suitor, a wealthy aristocrat and son of her late mistress, thinks that he can buy her and force her will. The aristocratic women think she is inso-lently proud because a female of her class is not expected to be virtuous. Furthermore, Pamela feels that her chasteness is necessary to preserve the meaning of her family. If she treats intercourse as a matter of gain or pleasure, then marriage and birth lose their meaning. Pamela is a good daughter surrounded by mothers. Her mistress educated her, and Mrs Jervis serves as her protector and confidante. Pamela's piety is also con-sistent with her goodness. She understands herself as a humble servant of God.

It is appropriate that *La Nouvelle Héloïse* imitates the form of *Pamela* more than any other work because goodness is its most fundamental characteristic. At the end of the novel, Rousseau tells the reader why the letters are agreeable to his taste:

> In having reread this collection, I believe to see why the interest, weak as it is, is so agreeable to me, and will be, I think, to every reader of a good nature. It is that, at least, this weak interest is pure and without a mixture of pain; that it is not excited by villainies, by crimes, nor mixed with the torment of hate. I cannot conceive what pleasure one can take in imagining and composing the person of a villain, to put oneself in his place, while one represents it, and to lend to him the most imposing brilliance. I pity much the authors of so many tragedies full of horror, who pass their lives making move and speak persons, whom one can-not listen to or see without suffering. It seems to me that one ought to bemoan being condemned to a task so cruel. Those who do it for amusement must be very devoured with zeal for the public utility. As for me, I admire, with a good heart, their talents and genius; but I thank God he has not given them to me.[59]

The romantic taste is not a taste for the satisfaction of justice. Punishing enemies or wrong doers with death or remorse, while pitying suffering virtue or exalting in its glorious victory is not romantic. Romanticism does not accompany involvement with those who do harm.

Yet, Julie is not as good as Pamela. She lies to her parents for the sake of love, and at one point, she wishes her mother were dead. Furthermore, she gives in to the weakness of her passions and thereby raises the question of female virtue in general, unlike Pamela, who is never tempted by love. Yet, on the side of the men, St. Preux is less criminal than Mr. B., Pamela's master and suitor. He goes so far as to kidnap and imprison Pamela, and to harm the preacher who wanted to help her. He is eventually redeemed by Pamela's suffering goodness and becomes her husband. *Pamela* is a more moral novel than *La Nouvelle Héloïse* because of the importance given to reforming the bad through the good.

Despite Pamela's suffering, the novel tends toward the comical. The only person to die is Mrs. B., and she has had a good and long life. Furthermore, we never meet her; her death opens the novel and removes a barrier to the main action. In *Pamela*, death is solved by birth. The letters end with an account of Pamela's deserved happiness as a wife and mother. The pains of unfulfilled longing and of loss do not set the tone of the whole work. The peace and serenity of family life dominate. This is in striking contrast to *La Nouvelle Héloïse*, where the heroine dies and the happiness of family life is called into question. Rousseau makes the family more of a problem than does Richardson by bringing passionate love and death into the picture. While Richardson does question the prejudices of the aristocracy by having Mr. B. fall in love with Pamela, he is sure to assimilate her into the old order, albeit an order slightly modified by virtue of allowing her entrance. Rousseau, on the other hand, has the daughter of a baron fall in love with an inconsiderable bourgeois. This conflicts with the ancestral patriarchy because the children belong to the male. The problems faced by Julie and St. Preux are much harder to work out than the problems of Pamela and Mr. B.

Pamela's death would serve no dramatic purpose other than to disturb the tranquillity of her family. Julie's death, to the contrary, is a dramatic necessity, which reveals the problems of her life and attempts to solve them. Julie dies at the end of the novel as a mother, wife, beloved, and daughter. Rousseau does not give in entirely to any one relation. She dies saving her son, her religion saves her husband from hell, her thoughts about heaven restore a hope for love that has lost its sweetness and taken on the character of belief, and her sons will be the continuation her father hoped for. The difficulty is with her relation as a friend, and one sees that Claire is the most inconsolable. The lover is consoled by an idea of heaven where he will be reunited in soul; the husband is consoled by the belief that she still exists in heaven; and the father is consoled because she lives on through her children. But, what about poor Claire? Death is more problematic for friends than any other relation. Friendship is a personal relation, like love and unlike familial relations. Husband and wife do not live to be with one another. They must please one another, but they are, first and foremost, the heads of the household and the cornerstone of society. Father and daughter is not a personal relation either; they do not choose one another. They are joined by birth, gratitude, and continuity. Friendship is personal, but, unlike love, it requires the bodily presence of the friend. The sighs of separated lovers are sweet, and they can be consoled by destiny. Heaven and earth seem to console everyone but friends.

Friendship precludes sexual intercourse and the concern with physical beauty, but it demands physical presence. Spiritedness is good for friendship because devotion is required where there is no physical pleasure. Bomston and Claire—the two friends in the novel—are, by far, the most spirited. The need for friends to be together is seen in the desire to bring Claire into the household at Clarens, once her husband has died. St. Preux is brought in only on the condition that he stop being a lover and become a friend. Claire also sleeps with Julie on her deathbed, and Julie dies in her arms.

Claire is the one most terrified and unconsoled by a dream of St. Preux's. He dreams that Julie was wearing a veil that could not be lifted, no matter how hard he tried. It is a premonition of her death, as there is no mutual recognition possible with the dead body itself. This need for the body and recognition of her dead friend drives Claire to the brink of madness. She becomes a protector of the dead body. She places a veil upon it and declares that whoever lifts the veil will be cursed. She can be cured from her near madness only by finding a reborn Julie on earth. This she finds in her own daughter. She loved her daughter before Julie's death, but never felt herself through her. She gladly allowed Julie to raise her. Friendship is, therefore, completed through birth, just as are the familial relations.

Pamela differs from *La Nouvelle Héloïse* not only in that it does not contain love and death; its depiction of familial serenity also differs. *Pamela* contains what Rousseau calls the English custom, where the two sexes live almost completely separately. In the second part of *Pamela*, we see such a way of living. Mr. B. leaves the estate in order to perform his parliamentary duties. The political life of England gives the sexes two different spheres and two very different tastes. Tenderness is difficult between them because of the male's political bent and the gulf between their occupations. Their relations are prosaic and citizenlike. At Clarens, on the other hand, the sexes work separately (although sometimes Julie actually joins Wolmar in overseeing the estate), but they both remain within the confines of the household. In *Pamela*, one of the great problems to overcome is Pamela's jealousy when her husband is away from home. In *La Nouvelle Héloïse*, it is Wolmar's jealousy that must be overcome when he invites St. Preux into the household. Wolmar only leaves the household to prove to his wife that she can trust herself and that, consequently, he is truly loved. He guards against the satiation of the senses by separating the sexes, but he also brings them close enough together to feel tenderness. His epicurean science of the household leaves little or no place for political concerns.

NOTES

1. Jean Jacques Rousseau, *Julie or The New Eloise*, translated and abridged by Judith H. McDowell (University Park, 1968).

2. Rousseau, Jean-Jacques. "Discourse on the Arts and the Sciences," in *The First and Second Discourses*. Trans. Roger Masters and Judith Masters, (1964, 34).

3. Rousseau, Jean-Jacques. *Emile*, trans. Bloom (1978, 39).

4. It is worth noting that contemporary cosmopolitans invented the term "politically correct" to describe themselves, which denotes polite behavior that does not offend as distinct from honest or just behavior.

5. Rousseau-Jean-Jacques, "Discourse on the Arts and Sciences," (1964, 33).

6. Rousseau, Jean-Jacques, *Letter to d'Alembert*, trans. Bloom, (1960, 30–31).

7. *La Nouvelle Héloïse* (Pléiade, 1964), II, xiv, p. 231.

8. Ibid., II, xiv, xvii, xxi, xxiii.

9. St. Preux does not discuss the character of the Parisian household in these letters. He discusses it later as a foil to Wolmar's household at Clarens (V, ii). The Parisian households are either tyrannies which keep order through fear and force, or they are anarchies, where everyone goes his own way, often at the expense of the master. Clarens is an attempt to combine order with freedom.

10. *Letter to d'Alembert*, pp. 34–47.

11. *La Nouvelle Héloïse*, II, xvi, p. 243.

12. Ibid., II, xvii, p. 246.

13. Ibid., II, xiv, p. 232.

14. Ibid., p. 231. Translations are my own.

15. Ibid., p. 232.

16. Ibid., p. 233.

17. Id.

18. Ibid., p. 235.

19. Bloom's analysis of Paris fails to examine its character as a gynaecocracy. In his introduction to the *Letter to d'Alembert*, he treats the arts of amusement as pleasantries belonging to a society that has lost the taste for freedom and virtue, but he does not look at it as having a distinctive character that reflects the nature of its rulers.

20. *La Nouvelle Héloïse*, II, xvii, p. 248.

21. Ibid., II, xvii, p. 250.

22. Ibid., p. 249.

23. Id.

24. Id.

25. Ibid., p. 251.

26. Id.

27. Ibid., p. 252.

28. Ibid., II, xxiii, p. 282.

29. *Emile*, p. 324.

30. *La Nouvelle Héloïse*, II, xvii, p. 253.

31. Ibid., p. 254.

32. *Letter to d'Alembert*, p. 47.

33. Id.

34. Ibid., p. 52.

35. Ibid., p. 55.

36. Id.

37. Ibid., p. 48.

38. Id.

39. *La Nouvelle Héloïse*, II, xxi, p. 267.

40. Ibid., II, xxvi, p. 294.

41. Abbé Prévost, *Memoirs of a Man of Honour*, (New York, 1975), p. 49. The name of the prostitute in Prévost's novel is also Fan-chon.

42. *La Nouvelle Héloïse*, II, xxi, p. 269.

43. Ibid., p. 271.

44. Id.

45. Id.

46. Id.

47. Id.

48. Ibid., p. 272.

49. Ibid., p. 276.

50. In the *Letter to d'Alembert*, p. 89, Rousseau says that force and submission without modesty is a return to northern barbarism, when the army traveled with their women. Novels of chivalry are romanticized versions of these relations.

51. *La Nouvelle Héloïse*, II, xxiii, p. 281.

52. Ibid. In V, vii, St. Preux describes the festivities of the grape harvest. There is singing and dancing, and St. Preux compares it to a spectacle. It is clearly meant to be compared to the Parisian opera. In fact, the letter begins with comments about how city people do not enjoy the pleasures of the country, even when they go there. While the opera is empty pomp, the grape harvest temporarily restores man to a more natural community. Music is perverse when it attempts to support pride. The nature of music requires that one give up oneself; it breaks down the barriers of class and creates a community among those who share in its god. At the harvest, there is the joy of being at one with humanity and nature. St. Preux praises unison in song and blames harmony.

53. *Emile*, p. 347.

54. Ibid., p. 343.

55. Ibid., p. 53.

56. *La Nouvelle Héloïse*, I, xxiii, p.79.

57. *Letter to d'Alembert*, p. 82. "I have made special mention of the English because they are, of all nations of the world, the one in which the morals of the two sexes appear, at first glance, to be most contrary." The letter on Geneva is VI, v.

58. Abbé Prévost, *Manon Lescaut*, trans. Tancock (New York, 1949), p. 23.

59. *La Nouvelle Héloïse*, VI, xiii, p. 745.

TWO

Rousseau's Romantic Reform of Christian Piety, Aristocratic Honor, and Patriarchal Authority

Love and family are alternatives not only to Paris, the Upper Valais, and Geneva, but to Vevey. Vevey is a small Swiss town, dominated by Julie's father Baron d'Etange. As reason, nature, and civic virtue dominated the other societies, God dominates Vevey. There, virtue and piety do not cluster around philosophy or country, but around obedience to the authority of fathers. Julie and St. Preux are Rousseau's Adam and Eve, who fall into disobedience by following their senses. Rousseau's romanticism undertakes a reform of the spirit, in addition to reforms of this world.

There is a novel that corresponds to Vevey, just as *Pamela* and *Manon Lescaut* correspond to the three other societies. Rousseau elsewhere called this novel by far the greatest novel ever written.[1] *Clarissa* is the story about a disobedient daughter whose virtue and piety raise her above the authority of her father and the villainy of her suitor. It is a very Christian work in so far as her virtue and piety require otherworldly devotion. Clarissa is much more sublime than Pamela. While Pamela's chastity served to defend humanity and family, Clarissa's chastity is meant to vindicate the entire female sex against fathers who broker marriages for money and rakes who do not believe in the possibility of female virtue. Her calling is a very high one. It shows the aristocratic face of Christianity, rather than that of the flock.

At first glance, Rousseau's disagreements with Richardson seem to be about public edification. He faults Richardson with attempting to correct the morals of a corrupt society with examples too exalted for their imitation.[2] Furthermore, the criticism made against Prévost, with respect to teaching moderation through tragedy, can also be made against Richardson. In *Clarissa*, he claims to teach parents and daughters to moderate their obstinacy to avoid catastrophe. But, he admits in the postscript that his tragedy will teach no such thing. The postscript is a defense of tragedy against the idea of poetic justice, which has taken hold of the fair sex. They do not want to see Clarissa die because she is virtuous and good. One sees in the postscript a possible source for St. Preux's observations on the decency of Parisian tragedy. Richardson says that he is teaching the principles of Christianity because Clarissa "dies happy." She meets the destiny for which she had a premonition and for which she prepared herself. This is not, however, a teaching of moderation.

The ineffectiveness of teaching morality to a corrupt people helps to reveal the irony of Rousseau's statement that the writers of tragedy must be moved by a zeal for the public utility. They are actually indulging their tastes under the guise of moral edification. Richardson clearly does not believe his own justifications. But, what about Rousseau's justifications to the public for *La Nouvelle Héloïse*? In the first preface, Rousseau claims that his novel will be more helpful to those girls who need guidance because it speaks directly to the love interest. He says that the love interest will not corrupt because any girl who reads the title and does not put the book down is already corrupt. Furthermore, the love story is not without moral difficulties. There are conflicts between innocence and love, virtue and love, reputation and love, death and love, and the good order of society and love. Rousseau forces anyone reading the novel to test all to which they are attached, by creating situations where one risks losing what is dearest. In addition to these conflicts, Rousseau follows the love story with a story about marriage and family.

It would be a mistake, however, to think that his novel was meant to correct the morals of the Parisians. He does say that a corrupt people can, at best, hope to raise themselves to the level of love, but he makes no claim to be their muse. He says that his book can, at best, preserve the goodness of peasants by making them content with their condition. He justifies literature to a corrupt people by saying that it gives them less time to devote to their vices, and that the pleasures of entertainment make them less vicious.[3] Rousseau's final justification for his novel is to himself. It is more in accord with his thought to understand him as affecting a new taste rather than as a reformer of corrupt morals.

While Manon was characterized by her charms, and Pamela by her goodness, Clarissa is distinguished by her virtue. Clarissa does not awaken in Lovelace, her adversary, feelings of love and humanity. It is not aristocratic pride and prejudice, as it was with Mr. B., that is Lovelace's vice. Clarissa must overcome a man whose experience with women has been one of betrayal and pleasureable disdain. He once believed in them, but has lost faith. His hate, contempt, and enjoyment has ripened into a creed—the rake's creed. He believes that no woman is truly virtuous and pious. This creed is accompanied by a mission—to confirm the truth of the creed by getting the most virtuous woman to be his mistress. His creed should not be mistaken as simply misogynous, although there is an element of that. Lovelace is humourously vain. He is splendidly handsome, and without equal in intellect and the duel. His conquests confirm his vain opinion of himself, as well as his ungenerous opinion of the opposite sex.[4] Clarissa is placed in the position of having to vindicate her sex. *Clarissa* is classed as a Christian/aristocratic tragedy.

Stendhal, a great admirer of *La Nouvelle Héloïse*, has made two remarks about *Clarissa* that help to characterize it. On an occasion when he was given to the praise of love, he called *Clarissa* a long and boring book because it contains so little of it.[5] He thought Clarissa proud, rather than modest. He finds fault with her for refusing Lovelace's hand in marriage after the rape rather than for feeling herself unworthy of marriage because she was raped. Love clearly takes a backstage to virtue and piety.

On another occasion, when Stendhal did not give himself over to love, he said of *Clarissa*:

> I shall love, I shall be in love with, I shall kneel down and worship and adore *Clarissa*, which, in my eyes, stands among the most beautiful, the most powerful, the most godlike achievements of the spirit of man; I shall yield to the exaltation and the rapture distilled from every drop of beauty, which dwells in the deep abundance of this strange masterpiece.[6]

No one could say this about *La Nouvelle Héloïse* because its heroine is not sublime, not even in her death. Clarissa, on the other hand, is exalted in life and death. She is an example of the sublimity of suffering virtue. Her suffering is sublime, rather than stoic, because it is accompanied by an opinion of her worthiness and the hope that she will meet with her exalted destiny. In *La Nouvelle Héloïse*, worthiness and destiny belong to the pains of love, but suffering love can never be exalted because it longs for bodily togetherness.

The suffering which Clarissa must endure is, above all, the suffering of injustice. She is subjected to the tyrannical will of her father and the villainy of Lovelace. The character of the novel depends on the interplay between her and her oppressors, especially the latter. Lovelace is continually torn between his love and admiration for Clarissa, and his creed and pride. He is like an angry and jealous god in his demand that she betrays family for him, and he is also like the devil in that he cleverly tests and tempts virtue and piety to win a victory that is resentful and malicious rather than righteous and glorious. Yet, the smallness of his scheming and the injustice of his demands make themselves felt to him through Clarissa's nobility of soul. Her love of the good and the honorable makes him feel what is for him the greatest pain—the awareness of his own inferiority. He vacillates between wanting to punish her for the pain she causes him and giving her the love and admiration she deserves.

Clarissa eventually embraces death. She cannot tolerate the prospect of being married to an unseemly man whose only recommendation is money, nor can she tolerate the schemes of a rake who wants to turn her into a mistress. She forsakes the world as it has forsaken her. The abuses she has encountered in life force her to seek her rewards in heaven. As she was above hatred in life, so is she in death. The injustices she suffers do not corrode her soul; she does not even find satisfaction in the thought that Lovelace will be punished in the afterlife, or that he will feel guilty for his crimes against her once she is dead. She has learned the lesson of Job—her exemplar; she suffers patiently rather than righteously. Her patience is accompanied by the serenity of a heart that awaits its exalted destiny. Her promised happiness, which will be more glorious than sad or sentimental, gives her the strength to forgive her malefactors, and to become almost indifferent to them. Her death conquers Lovelace. Her superiority of soul can no longer be odious to him now that she is dead. She is owed his pity and admiration and he must confront his own baseness and crimes. He is challenged to a duel by Colonel Morden, Clarissa's uncle, where he receives the deadly blow for which he sought. His last words are a cry for expiation.

Richardson's novel is a tragedy and it is clearly the tragedy Rousseau had in mind when he spoke of lending imposing brilliance to villains and crimes. Lovelace is the most charming and brilliant villain that one could ever imagine. We cannot forget that Clarissa hoped to be able to love him had he proven good and virtuous, and that one of Richardson's edifying purposes is to warn against an adage that the best husband is a reformed rake. The beauty of the tragedy requires the satisfaction of justice. Richardson answers the complaint of the fair sex that his novel must satisfy justice by saying that it does.

> These are the great authorities so favourable to the stories that end unhappily; yet, the writer of *The History of Clarissa* is humbly of the opinion that he might have been excused for referring to them for the vindication of his catastrophe, even by those who are of the contrary opinion; since the notion of *poetical justice*, founded on the *modern rules*, has hardly ever been more strictly observed in works of this nature, than in the present performance, if any regard at all be paid to the *Christian system* on which it is formed.
>
> For is not Mr Lovelace, who could persevere in his villainous views, against the strongest and most frequent convictions and remorses that ever were sent to awaken and reclaim a wicked man; is not this great, this wilful transgressor, condignly punished. . . . And who that are earnest in their profession of Christianity, but will rather envy than regret the triumphant death of Clarissa, whose piety from her early childhood, whose diffusive charity, whose steady virtue, whose Christian humility, whose forgiving spirit, whose meekness, whose resignation, HEAVEN *only* could reward.[7]

Punishment and reward are essential to tragedy, and, in *Clarissa*, we see a Christian distribution of them.

La Nouvelle Héloïse also tells the history of a young lady, but her history is different from Clarissa's in that it is far from being a traditional tragedy. It is even more sentimental and humane than the tragedies of Euripides. Rousseau's novel fails the first test of tragedy by not presenting characters who are clearly greater than ourselves. As Bomston says,

> It is not that either of you have a marked characteristic by which, at first glance, one can distinguish you, and it could very well be that this difficulty in defining you might cause a superficial observer to take you for common souls. But it is this very thing that distinguishes you, that it is impossible to differentiate you, and the features of the common model, of which some are always lacking in each individual, all shine equally in you.[8]

Not only are the leading characters not of tragic greatness, but the novel as a whole fails to produce the tragic fear that is in excess of pity. Tragedy produces fear and pity because it has as its subject the breaking of divine law. The suffering of an innocent victim evokes pity, and the violence of the crime and the fear of punishment cause fear. Guilt is testimony to the moral nature of the world. Rousseau states that his novel may evoke pity, but not fear.[9] The awe one feels in front of great crimes and horrible, violent sufferings is absent in *La Nouvelle Héloïse*, as well as the awe that one feels in witnessing virtue's strength. Rousseau's novel does not contain the heights and depths that cause a striking effect; Rousseau replaces the striking with the tender. Bomston serves as a commentator on the novel when he says,

> There are neither intrigues, nor adventures in what you have recounted to me . . . and yet, the catastrophes of a novel would interest me much less, so much do your sentiments take the place of its situations and your honest behaviour that of its striking action. Your two souls are so extraordinary that one cannot judge them by common rules. Happiness is for you neither on the same route, nor of the same kind as that of other men; they seek only power and the looks of others, but you need only tenderness and peace.[10]

The replacement of the striking with the tender means that the satisfaction of justice is not at the core of the novel as it is in *Clarissa*. That is not to say that injustice triumphs, but that no injustice is committed that calls for a rain of punishments. *La Nouvelle Héloïse* is less moral than *Clarissa* because it is more sympathetic to love. The only thing less agreeable to love than anger is indifference.

The movement away from the striking toward the tender is reflected in the different appearances between Julie and St. Preux on the one hand, and Clarissa and Lovelace on the other. Both Clarissa and Lovelace are of godlike beauty. Their beauty is known through its effect, which is to make those that see them stop and stare in admiration. Certainly, their physical beauty accounts for a great deal of the attraction between them. Their beauty corresponds to the intelligence and heroic qualities they possess, and that is expected from their appearance. Julie and St. Preux, on the other hand, are not of the greatest imaginable beauty. Each declares that the other could be physically more attractive.[11] They are better than average, but they are not images of the divine. Their appearances promise a tender and permanent attachment. Everyone would be struck by Clarissa's beauty, but those without sensitive souls might not give Julie a second glance.

St. Preux and Julie will read Plutarch in order to see the sublime and rare virtues, but they will not exhibit the same strengths.[12] There is nothing impressive about their bodies or their accomplishments. What makes them exceptional is their elevated sentiment. The tests they are confronted with are the tests of sensitive souls. Julie must choose between love and the attachment to her parents. She must probe her heart and understanding to make her decisions. There is little of the doubtless intrepidity and single-minded devotion that inspires overwhelming admiration and even awe. There are no spectacles of heroic courage and Christian piety to set the tone of the novel. The tenderness of romantic love—the memory of a lost happiness that still touches, because it is accompanied by real, if ill-defined, hopes—determines the poetic character of the novel as a whole.

The replacement of the striking with the tender is also part of Rousseau's reform of religious authority. The book of Job—the book that teaches Clarissa about the meaning of her suffering and of her devotion—teaches that awe is the recognition of God's incomprehensible character, the proof of his existence, and the unquestionableness of his authority. Job was thought to be presumptuous for suffering righteously. He took it upon himself to defend God's justice. God is beyond man's understanding of justice. His authority is made known through the speechless terror and awe that is inspired by his acts, both creative and destructive. The restoration of Job from his suffering is not an act of justice, but of benevolence. Job has no claim to be benefited. Obedience ought to be from reverential love rather than from justice and expectation. But, of course, Job is more than restored in terms of his prosperity.

Rousseau's sentimental reform of tragedy is a reform of religious instinct and understanding. We cannot forget that tragedy belongs to the Greek polis, that the fear and pity it evokes speaks to the religious sentiments and understanding of the citizenry.[13] Tragedy is meant to support and interpret religion. Rousseau's replacement of terror and awe with tender love and tender pity attenuates the character of authority that compels belief through fear and trembling. Rousseau's weakening of traditional authority paves the way for a natural religion that moves from sentiment and observation to belief. A natural religion is a more tolerant religion for the most obvious reason that it is not sectarian. If God is known through observation and sentiment, then the hatreds of sects, based on different scriptures and different scriptural authorities, become less violent and even dissipate altogether. Even more important, as the example of Wolmar shows, is that a natural religion can tolerate atheists, not atheists who proclaim disbelief to distinguish themselves or to justify their pleasures and selfishness, but virtuous atheists whose minds do not consent to belief (philosophers). There is no hell in Julie's natural religion. A natural religion would not hold philosophic disbelief to be disobedient and heretical; it would find tolerance in the confidence that atheism is insupportable, and that the philosopher, who has the faculties to believe, will come to believe. The conversion of Wolmar is the final promise of the novel and the fulfilment of Julie's prayers. The novel, as a whole, justifies natural religion and is, therefore, a judicious combination of reason and belief. Although, one cannot but wonder whether Wolmar is truly a philosopher.

While the form of the novel and the form of the title imitate Richardson, the title itself points directly to the life of Heloïse. Héloïse is different from Clarissa and similar to Julie in that she loved her lover (Abelard) more than she loved virtue and God. The reference to Héloïse is consistent with a break from Richardson, but Julie is La Nouvelle Héloïse, as opposed to the old Héloïse. If she resembles Héloïse in her fall, she does not resemble her in her redemption. Julie becomes a wife and mother. She does not enter a convent as did Héloïse. Julie combines redemption with earthly attachments. Her devotion to God perfects the imperfection of her attachments without demanding that she give them up completely. Her natural religion is a consequence of her inability to believe that a just God would punish Wolmar. She even hopes to be reunited with St. Preux in heaven, which is actually a sanctuary for unhappy lovers. Héloïse was unhappily divided between obedience to God and her love of Abelard. Rousseau, recognizing the strength of earthly attachments, reforms religion to accord with them.

Romanticism is a reform not only of the female, but also of the male. The most obvious reform is that of the saint. Julie's lover, St. Preux, is the only saint in the novel. He earns his name by proving his love for Julie, not for God.[14] St. Preux is Rousseau's romantic hero who sacrifices his happiness for love. St. Preux is to Abelard, as Julie is to Héloïse. He finds redemption in devotion to Julie's memory and in the hope of returning to her, whereas Abelard gives himself to God, once he is cut off from Héloïse. The sensualization of Christianity is also evident in Rousseau's use of a quotation from Petrarch: "the world possessed her without knowing her, and me, I knew her, I remain below to mourn for her."[15] Rousseau places the quotation on his title page as a comprehensive remark about the whole work, whereas Petrarch makes the statement with a view to renouncing it. As Petrarch approaches death, he realizes that

God alone is worthy of devotion. He forgets Laura, and counts the eleven years he spent mourning her as a mistake. Even his love of Laura is less sensual than St. Preux's love of Julie; it was not even consummated with a kiss. The unattainable and other worldly is more prominent in Petrarch than in romanticism.

St. Preux's sacrifices make him an alternative to the heroic tradition and philosophy as well. The prospect of a duel between St. Preux and Bomston, a great lord of England, provides the opportunity for subordinating the heroic to love. The replacement of admiration for the heroic is most apparent in the portrayal of Bomston. He has a reputation throughout Europe as a superior dueler, and he is a brave and patriotic soldier. But, we do not see him kill for his honor or defend and lead an empire or a free people. The treatment of Bomston helps us understand Rousseau's romantic reform of aristocratic honor and, to a lesser extent, that of pagan heroism. Rousseau allows us to admire his heroism only once; that action is portrayed in one of the engravings entitled *l'heroism de valeur*. In that instance, Bomston compels the admiration of those around him by confessing his injustice (he insulted Julie while drunk) and asking forgiveness from St. Preux, whom he considers Julie's representative. His heroism is that of a great man who, without fear for his reputation, is willing to admit he has done wrong and places himself at the discretion of another (in this case, St. Preux, a poor bourgeois who is not his social equal). Bomston is to serve as an example to others that there is no honor in a courage that is lacking in justice and probity.

Bomston's plea for forgiveness is the resolution of what was to be a duel to the death. The resolution takes place on account of Julie's intervention. She is both the source of the strife and the cause of its peaceful conclusion. The influence she has in the matter reflects the elevation of women at the expense of the heroic in general. The bending of Bomston's knee is the defeat of heroism and the victory of romantic love. Courage belongs to love in *La Nouvelle Héloïse*. The soldier has lost the ground on which to display the most impressive virtues. Bomston wins admiration, not through his courage, but through his generosity to the lovers. Yet, even his generosity is subordinated to love. He feels guilty for having slandered Julie, and he wants her respect for himself, as well as her own happiness. The resolution of the duel has great implications for the poetic tradition.

The possibility of a duel between St. Preux and Bomston prompts Julie's reflections on it as an institution. She writes a letter to St. Preux in an attempt to persuade him to lay down his arms.[16] Julie says that the reason for the duel is honor; it is a way to seek satisfaction against an insult to oneself, or what is dearest to oneself. She tries to relieve St. Preux from his anger through ridicule, argument, and humanity, not love. She will not speak of what love requires, because love clearly demands a duel. Nor will she use the authority granted to her by St. Preux to forbid the duel. She was, however, willing to use that authority earlier in a matter concerning what he perceived to be his honor. She ordered him to accept money from her upon his trip through the Alps. She considered his refusal of the money to be obstinate pride rather than honor. The wealth of lovers is in common; they cannot have the pride that comes from independence. Julie's refusal to use her authority on the occasion of the duel reveals that she thinks the honor of love requires a fight. It is not surprising that the resolution of the duel requires that Bomston, rather than St. Preux, be persuaded to lay down his arms. Aristocratic pride and honor give way to love.

Julie's attempt to persuade St. Preux through ridicule, argument, and sentiment are meant to prove that the honor at issue in the duel has neither justice, nor goodness, nor truth on its side and is, therefore, false honor. She ridicules St. Preux's indignation by asking him if the way to avenge oneself is to allow oneself to be killed, for it is certain that Bomston will be victorious. Indignation is ridiculous when it is too weak to even hope to exact punishment. But, it is not honorable to give in to ridicule; there can be truth in a losing cause. Julie, therefore, turns to truth, justice, and goodness to persuade St. Preux.

Julie's arguments against the duel get their force from the examples of the ancients. Plutarch and Plato are her authorities. Roman civic virtue, as embodied in Brutus and Cato, and Greek philosophy, as embodied in Socrates, are her examples of true honor. She says that the duel was unknown to the ancients, that it belongs to the Christian aristocracy. The justice of the duel is not the justice of the ancient republic, or even of the tribe. Avenging an insult is different from avenging injustice. Honor, which is more personal than justice, is the spring of the duel. If the honor of a duel is to be linked with justice, then, it is with the justice of the biblical God, who is a proud and jealous God, a destroyer of blasphemers. In the case of man, the replacement of honor for law leads to the justice of wolves, rather than to the enforcement of the divine code. The code of honor honors the sword, because there is no authority beyond it. It is actually a very good custom for the elevation of scoundrels; they can challenge men of distinction with the sole intent of elevating themselves on the graves of the latter.

Not only does the duel not support justice, but it does not support the truth. The truth is not a question of force, nor is it subject to insult. Truth and justice are not personal; they are outside of the self. Julie puts a twist on the Socratic love of truth by speaking of it in terms of probity. She says that Socrates, as well as Cato, possessed good witness of themselves. True honor is informed by truth and justice; it does not depend on the opinion of others, nor is it a good that can be stolen.

Julie is not, however, aware of the radicalness of her arguments, for they suggest that a duel is never justified. If one's honor depends upon one's own goodness, then, it is beyond insult and vindication. But, she believes that duels can be justified and even admits that St. Preux has been insulted. Furthermore, she says that she could never love a coward.[17] Given the above, we are led to believe that her reflections on honor are not her deepest reasons for opposing the duel, but are meant to enable St. Preux to disengage himself without losing her respect. Julie reveals her more personal reasons against the duel at the end of the letter. These reasons are not publicly respectable because they concern neither honor, nor justice. She is horrified by the barbarity of it and is terrified by passions which could cause friends to kill one another.[18] Her terrors will eventually be the ground for a new order.

Julie knew her letter would be unpersuasive and that St. Preux's love would cause him to seek the deadly blow. Her letter is not even persuasive to herself. Love cannot survive unavenged insults. Julie suffers the dilemma of love. She would like St. Preux to live so that they can be happy together, but the bond that unites them would be compromised by putting their happiness first. Julie's hope to unite love and happiness depends on her persuasion of Bomston rather than St. Preux.

Julie's letter to Bomston does not speak of true honour, though one would think that those arguments are more appropriate for him. She does not use her sophistic arguments on him, but instead, makes him feel the injustice of killing with one blow two lovers, who only sought to honor him. Julie's letter is a success because he can beg forgiveness without seeming to be a coward or an inferior. His apology should not, however, be mistaken for generosity or probity, although it may appear so to those who witness it. Bomston bends his knee because he loves Julie; he made the insinuation that St. Preux enjoyed her attention because he was jealous of St. Preux. Bomston does not want to harm her or those she loves. It is true that once he learns that St. Preux is her lover, he renounces his love as a tender admiration without hope and declares himself unworthy because of his past affairs. Yet, his renunciation is not completely honest. He takes on the role of St. Preux's confidant and the spokesperson for the rights of love. He clings to what is dearest to Julie and does his best to make her dreams of love come true. His hopes are not annihilated, but finds consolation through her gratitude and admiration. The great lord is a disappointed lover who redeems himself by serving love. The hero must serve the cause of love or be without one.[19]

Although Julie's discussion of true honor is not persuasive to herself or to St. Preux, it requires examination because it reveals a conflict between love and reason. St. Preux reads Julie's letter with a mind to refute it because love is his only reason. It is up to the reader to undertake a detached examination of the issues. The conflict between love and reason is seen most clearly in the differences between St. Preux and Socrates. The virtue of Socrates is like that of a horse; it is independent of money and the opinion of others.[20] The virtue of his soul and the truth he seeks are not subject to insults, nor can they be vindicated by force. St. Preux's indignation indicates that his love is dearer to him than his life, but it also indicates that his love is dearer to him than philosophy. He says that, as long as he lives, he will force others to treat her with the respect he feels for her in his heart.[21] He vindicates Julie's honor, even though the insinuation was true because it threatens his faith. He cannot allow her to be blasphemed without losing the passionate faith that connects him to her. The spirit of his faith is not the spirit of philosophy.

St. Preux's faith in love is impressive because it accompanies generous sentiments and courageous action. But his love has a questionable side as is clear from Julie's criticisms. Love is a sublime self-indulgence from the perspective of philosophy. The supreme sacrifice is the sacrifice of oneself to the truth, to the insignificance of one's own particular existence. St. Preux's vindication of love is bound up with himself. He must believe that Julie's beauty is contained within herself, but by defending her against insult, he reveals that her beauty depends on him. Would the offence to her modesty be so painful and infuriating to him if her beauty were independent of his love? He wants to silence doubts about his faith and his god because his goodness and happiness depend upon his being worthy of his god. His happiness depends upon particular attachments, and his indignation must support those attachments.

Rousseau's romantic hero is not simply at odds with philosophy. He shares with Socrates an element of the natural that is not characteristic of the pagan hero. Both St. Preux and Socrates are foils to Cato. Cato is dependent upon the political community for his sense of honor. He must benefit it and respect its gods to attain his reward. St. Preux and Socrates are more immediately connected to the body and the mind, respectively. Rousseau's portrayal of love in terms of romantic love rather than philosophy is the consequence of his understanding of the primacy of the body. The shared activity of lovers is easily understood. Plato, on the other hand, teaches that true love is unreciprocated because nature cannot love. Socrates makes the sacrifice that St. Preux cannot make.

Equity is a great theme in romanticism because reciprocated love must be given a foundation where only the body is natural. Romanticism must sublimate nature in order to found a community on love. Philosophic friendship has none of the problems of equity faced by Rousseau because the goal, knowledge, can be shared without costing one friend more than another. Furthermore, the shared activity is a natural desire that brings the friends together without the requirement of moral justification. The virtues of romanticism, on the other hand, are clearly linked to the body; modesty and fidelity have much to do with the exclusive possession of one another's body, not only trust. The virtue of the philosopher does not depend on social virtues. The admiration for him has nothing to do with possessing him. Both Plato and Rousseau combine pleasure, community, and virtue, but the soul is Plato's centerpiece, while Rousseau's is the body.

The differences between Plato and Rousseau with respect to intellectual virtue are readily seen in the most elemental aspects of *La Nouvelle Héloïse*. The friendship between Wolmar, St. Preux, and Bomston has less to do with philosophy than with a shared, though different, love for Julie.[22] Furthermore, the entire novel is divided according to Julie's relation to men. The first part of the novel is about love, and the second is about marriage and family. These relations mirror the sexual and reproductive aspects of the body.

Although love is not philosophy, the lovers resemble Socrates in their understanding of justice and in their weakness. They think the first principle of justice is to do no harm.[23] They compromise with it, but they clearly believe that a lover should injure no one.[24] The opposite is true of the good citizen, who must harm enemies. The lovers, like Socrates, do not possess a claim to justice that can be a source of public anger and legitimate its force. A large part of the lovers' drama is their confrontation with justice, as it is embodied in the claims of fathers. They are unable to conquer the paternal force, although that force is modified through the course of the novel. Birth and death are facts of nature that give more force to the family and society than to lovers.

Romantic love is neither philosophy, nor nature, nor civic virtue. The pleasures of love are clearly natural in the sense that they are accompanied by a natural and complete bodily experience, but the pleasures of the body are elevated by sentiments and ideas, which inspire courage, sacrifice, and opinions about the true meaning of life. Love, however, is its own reward. The same cannot be said of civic virtue because it is not sweet. Love promises to relieve man from the imperfections of his existence by giving to him a complete satisfaction. Desire is satisfied; the partiality of existence is made whole; particularity is universalized through the experience of the beautiful, and the weight of mortality and sacrifice is lightened by the eternal truth and meaning of one's love. The classic alternative to civic virtue (philosophy) is equally removed from romantic love. Sacrifice, reward, and vindication belong to faith rather than to the intellectual virtue of philosophy. The universality of the mind does not require reciprocation and support from gods.

Just as Rousseau's romantic reform of female virtue corresponds to a reform of male virtue, so, too, the reform of female faith and obedience corresponds to a reform of male authority. The reform of male authority is seen most clearly in the substitution of Wolmar's regime for the baron's regime. The baron and Wolmar are paired together, as are Bomston and St. Preux; and, as Bomston gives way to St. Preux, Wolmar replaces the baron. Baron d'Etange is an example of the aristocracy that reads like a textbook on what Nietzsche says about it in its early stages.[25] He is concerned with honor above all else. His honor does not resemble vanity. He wants to be honored for what he is, or, at least, what he believes himself to be. His word is a matter of the greatest importance, because honesty is nobility. The nobleman must always be himself to be noble, and he must always be noble to be himself. Since the baron must be what he should be, he does not have to justify himself to others. He is more concerned with his honor than with the common good. He is confident that his will is beyond reproach. He, therefore, has the capacity to hate and to punish. The baron is not, however, a god on earth. He is conservative. The order to which he subordinates his will and that of others is not of his own making. Belief in the nobility of his ancestors is necessary to his opinion of himself.

Rousseau, like Nietzsche, believed that the Enlightenment destroyed the possibility of an aristocracy founded on tradition. The background of the entire novel is the decline of aristocracy and monarchy. The wars between nations have no religious meaning. The armies are made up of debauched mercenaries who are just another interest group. The French aristocracy has lost its independence from the monarchy, which is, in turn, fighting a war that it will lose to the British. The only light in which we see the British Empire is in its inhumanity to those who suffer under its yoke. The rest of the picture is filled out with Bomston's disgust for the English court, Wolmar's loss of his kingdom, and the vanity and license of the aristocracy living in Paris.

The picture of the aristocracy is not bleak simply because it is seen from the perspective of the charms of private life. The authority of the aristocracy itself is called into question. Rousseau differs greatly from Richardson by using private life to call the legitimacy of the aristocracy into question. Rousseau believes in the possibility of a rural aristocratic family without the authoritative prejudices of the aristocracy. In *Clarissa*, Richardson hopes to both moderate the obstinate authority of fathers and the obstinate love of daughters. He claims to teach moderation through tragedy. Clarissa's father and brother, James I and James II, play an important part in her death through their obstinacy, and Clarissa plays a part in her own demise because her attraction to Lovelace was in need of further judgement. Richardson never attacks the legitimacy of aristocracy as such. He does not propose the marriage between a noblewoman and a commoner, as does Rousseau. In *Pamela*, he only dares to marry a nobleman to a commoner. But, Rousseau pushes the legitimacy of the aristocracy to its limits by having Lord Bomston propose to Baron d'Etange the marriage of St. Preux to Julie. Rousseau also allows Bomston a vicious, but judicious, critique of aristocratic prejudice.[26] Marriage and family undergo a major transformation in Rousseau's hands. He is not, like Richardson, simply a moderator of authoritative excess.

Although Rousseau agrees with Nietzsche about the fate of aristocratic claims founded on tradition, he does not agree with him about the alternative. Nietzsche embraces the idea of a planetary aristocracy that rules with a good conscience, precisely because it rules in accord with the will to power. Nietzsche is so opposed to democracy that he turned his mind and rhetoric to the first condition of aristocracy; the affirmation of hierarchy through force is the essence of the will to power. For Nietzsche, the first step toward greatness is the subordination of women.[27] He encourages the use of force against them as a solution to egalitarian relations. Rousseau also wants to correct egalitarian relations between the sexes, and he also recognizes that force is the first law of nature, that the relations between the sexes must respect the superior strength of the male.[28] But, he does not welcome force. He attempts to sublimate it so that the male is protective of the female. The realm of love is where women rule men through affection rather than justice and force. Private life is the domain of woman.

The gentle and even invisible rule of Wolmar at Clarens is Rousseau's improvement of the rule of the baron at Vevey. The baron's marriage was without tenderness. As a young husband and father he went into the army where he took mistresses. He returns home for support in his old age only to demand that his daughter marry his friend in order to pay a debt of gratitude. The baron is the closest thing in the novel to a tyrant and a villain.

Rousseau reforms the meaning of paternal authority just as he reformed the meaning of heroism. As he presents an engraving of the newly understood valor of the hero, he presents an engraving of the newly understood force of the father (accompanied by the subscript "la force paternelle"). And as he showed us an image of a hero kneeling before a poor bourgeois asking for forgiveness, he shows us a father kneeling before his daughter begging for pity. One cannot underestimate the importance of the situation. The scene is the culmination between the conflict between love and paternal authority, and it prepares the ground for the conflict between love with marriage and family.

Julie's father told her she was to marry Wolmar some three years before the marriage. She does not, however, rebel against his command until Wolmar's return is announced and the marriage seems imminent. The arrival of Wolmar destroys her hope and trust in fate. For the first time in her life she openly disobeys her father and discovers that her love has made her more obstinate than him. Unable to force her through authority, he falls to his knees and begs Julie not to send him to his grave as she did her mother. He conquers her will, though not her heart, through guilt and pity.

The conquest must be understood in light of previous failures to resolve the conflict. In the first crisis, the baron arrives home from the army and tells her she is to marry Wolmar. This order is given after Julie and St. Preux have kissed and when they have separated from fear of the passion that consumes them. The crisis reaches a boiling point when St. Preux threatens suicide because he cannot live in his condition. He must possess her (or, at least, be given a definite promise of possession), or he must put an end to himself. He will mend his life or be rid of it. Unable to resolve the conflict, Julie is incapacitated. She becomes ill and hopes to die. Her friend Claire begs St. Preux to save her. Upon arriving, St. Preux asks Julie to elope. Unable to abandon her parents and unable to wound her lover, she abandons virtue to preserve all else.

She hopes that love will supply the solution to its own evil by producing a child. She wants to use her father's concern with honor, reputation, and continuity against him. She thinks that, in order to avoid a scandal and to have a legitimate heir, the baron would give her to her lover. Rousseau makes clear that he could have resolved the conflict in this way and, like Molière, given a victory to the lovers over the father. But, Rousseau decides that the plot will not work itself out after Julie's plan because he does not unambiguously side with love. He recognizes the importance of attachments that are formed around reproduction. A lesser writer might have resolved the conflict according to Julie's plan and, thereby, denied us the opportunity to see the conflict between love and parental attachment played out to its limits. Rousseau forces Julie to live the conflict without the help of a *deus ex machina*.

The character of the conflict is seen most vividly when Bomston attempts to be a *deus ex machina*. Love looks defeated. The baron has forbidden Julie to see and to write to St. Preux. Furthermore, there are rumors that they are lovers. St. Preux is banished by Claire in order to preserve Julie's reputation and in order to protect Julie from a love without hope. Bomston, who is responsible for the pitch of the crisis, seeks to remedy the harm by offering Julie the opportunity for happiness. He offers to take her to England where she can marry St. Preux with the sanction of the law. Bomston sweetens the offer by guaranteeing her safety from her father and by providing them with a rural estate. Julie refuses Bomston's offer because love alone cannot bring her happiness. She could not be happy knowing that she has driven her parents into hopeless despair. She is their only living child, their hope for the continuity of their name and themselves. Julie says that to drive them to despair amounts to killing them. The horror of the crime restrains her and, thereby, takes the place of abandoned innocence and virtue.

One might argue that the horror of driving her parents to despair does not mark the true limit of her soul because she hopes that her father will give her to St. Preux if he should make a fortune and distinguish himself while in Paris and London. Perhaps, the hope to resolve the conflict speaks louder than her horror. But, the final confrontation with her father confirms that her horror marks her limitation. The horror and pity Julie experiences upon her father's plea reminds one of the catharsis of a tragedy. He tries to make her feel guilty for her mother's death and, thereby, receive the benefits of purgation for himself. She cannot look at death with a dry eye, precisely because it is so horrible. Pity is a mode of mourning that is a consolation because it overcomes the indifference of death. One cannot pity what is insensible. Her father is obeyed, but it is from the force of humanity rather than the force of authority.

Although Julie has learned what she must give to her father, she has not learned to reconcile the claims of the father with the claims of the lover. Why should not the lover present an image of death that cannot be tolerated any more than the death of a father? Rousseau, in fact, follows the tragedy of the patricide with the tragedy of the lovers. After having given her consent to marry Wolmar, Julie takes ill with smallpox. St. Preux hears of her illness and travels days without rest to see her. It is on this occasion that he receives his pseudonym. He lives up to his name by inoculating himself with kisses. Unable to cure her, he hopes to share her death.

Julie is in a state of half-consciousness when St. Preux inoculates himself. Upon her recovery, she finds herself tormented by the memory of his arrival, which she mistakes for a dream so vivid and recurring as to be prescient of their fate. Claire, fearing Julie's sanity, imprudently tells her the truth about the incident and about St. Preux's pitiful condition. Julie is too weak to resist love. St. Preux is the truest of lovers, according to Julie, because his love survived hope. She cannot be indifferent to his sufferings any more than she could be indifferent to her father's sufferings. Unable to resolve her conflicting attachments, she and St. Preux contemplate adultery. Her solution is worth reflecting upon because it is an attempt to satisfy two conflicting passions. She could avoid the horror of death and pay her debt to love by being an adulteress. She does not fear adultery, not because she has reason on her side, but because she is overwhelmed by passion. Julie's reason falls into a state of atrophy because it cannot reconcile her contradictory sentiments with an opinion about virtue and justice. She walks up the marriage aisle with adultery in her heart and lies in her mouth. One sees here the inspiration for Scott's and Donizetti's brides of Lammermoor. But, Julie's wedding is not the scene of her tragedy, although some might think she were better dead. She undergoes a change of heart and mind as she walks up the aisle, and, when she takes her vows she is sincere.

Julie's conversion is treated as a return to God. She now believes, whereas before, she mouthed the words. The return to God is described by her as a relief from a state of barbarism. The barbaric state is one where there is no order. Rousseau says that the desire for intercourse and the horror of death are the primordial passions of civilized man that need to be educated.[29] By bringing love and paternal authority into conflict with one another, Rousseau, through Julie, brings us back to a distinctly human, but primitive, condition. It is worth noting that this condition of life without order has much in common with life in Paris.

Julie's awakening from the atrophy of reason takes place in the church. As she walks down the aisle she sees friends and family. Most notably, she sees Claire with her husband M. d'Orbe, who presents to her an image of peace and tranquillity. These impressions leave their mark. She feels the possibility of being restored to a place; the law she is restored to confirms that place. Her vow is that of a girl who has lost her way and who recoils at the abyss. In the midst of her stupidity and terror, she finds strength in blind and loving obedience. She is restored to God, family, and friends. The law that emerges from her confrontation with barbarism is Rousseau's romantic credo. It is not blind and loving obedience to either God or husband, but the belief in the sacredness of marriage. The prohibition against adultery is Julie's first commandment; belief in God is even a secondary and derivative matter.

Julie's barbarity and return to civilization is in striking contrast to Hobbes and to Christianity. In his state of nature, Hobbes concentrates the imagination on death, but it is the fear of one's own violent death at the hands of another, rather than despair from the death of one's abandoned father. Rousseau attempts to awaken a horror that seeks relief in a moral relation, whereas Hobbes awakens a horror that can be solved through calculation and contract.

Rousseau also avoids the path of Christianity with respect to death. The horror of death is understood by Christianity as the horror of punishment that can be avoided if one denies oneself the pleasures of the body. According to Rousseau, Christianity makes man cruel because the horror of hell, combined with the denial of the body, issues forth in a love of God that is not infrequently satisfied by punishing sinners.[30]

Julie does not absorb herself in the fear of humans, nor does she absorb herself in the fear of God. Consequently, she does not look toward the fear of a civil sovereign or the fear of God for relief from the fear of humans, nor does she look toward the fear of humans or the desire to punish them in order to relieve herself from the fear of God. She fears death in its finality, but that finality is made sensible to her through the prospect of the ingratitude and indifference of children toward the lives of their parents, and the consequent despair of their parents. She fears to feed on horrors that would make her callous to life, for she feels that the connection between parent and child is fundamental, that there is no justice that would obliterate that connection. She is incapable of internalizing the necessity of death as would an atheist. But, her failure to internalize that necessity does not drive her mind into a narrow concern with keeping her body alive. Nor does she spend her life sinning, repenting, and punishing because she is torn between her desires and the terrors of hell.

Husband and wife present an image of holy union. Marriage is an affirmation of a trust that is more than a mercenary contract, an avowal of love, or a pledge of obedience. They vow before God, themselves, and their family and friends. The sacredness of their vows is connected to procreation. Husband and wife are not complete in themselves. Their union contains within it a glimpse of a larger whole. Marriage is only the family in potentiality. The separate bodies of husband and wife find unity and continuity in children. Marriage is a bridge from the individual to society.

After Julie's marriage, she writes St. Preux a letter that refutes the sophistic opinion that adultery harms no one.[31] This opinion is that of the enlightened in Paris, and St. Preux uses them as an authority when trying to convince himself and Julie that adultery is not wrong. She reminds him of his own rebukes of the wise men of Paris, and she quotes to him his own words:

> Love is deprived of its greatest charm when honesty is abandoned. In order to sense its entire worth, it is necessary that the heart comply with it, and that it elevate us in elevating the loved object. Take away the idea of perfection, and you take away enthusiasm. Take away esteem and love is no longer anything. How will a woman honor a man she ought to despise? How will she be able to honor herself, the one who does not fear to abandon herself to a vile corrupter? Thus, they will soon despise one another. Love, the celestial sentiment, will no longer be for them anything but a shameful commerce. They will have lost honor, and will have not found happiness.[32]

How far they have fallen. Two lovers, who once found virtue necessary for love, come to the point of finding their salvation in adultery. Julie does not understand this fall as a mere accident. She denounces love as an illusion, which mistakes sensuality for virtue. It is no wonder that St. Preux's letters on Paris never discussed the relation of the love interest in the drama to the family and civic virtue. There has never been a society of lovers because lovers belong to one another exclusively. Love cannot even accommodate children into its circle. It is a rebel when considered from the perspective of marriage and family, and that is the perspective Julie now takes.

Julie's horror at the crime of adultery stems more from the tragedy of the patricide than the tragedy of lovers. The sacredness of marriage and the law against adultery ensure that the death of fathers is a matter of importance, much more even than the fate of the lover. In fact, Julie's letter causes St. Preux to contemplate suicide and to seek death at sea. The guilt disturbs her, but does not crush her. The guilt of a patricide is much more unbearable for her because she expects to have children of her own. When she refused Bomston's offer to take her to England, she said that it would be self-defeating to have children after having driven her own parents to despair. Even as a young girl in love, she lives in relation to the children she has yet to have given birth to. The relation she has to her parents is inextricably bound to her relation to her own children. When reflecting upon the evils of adultery, she imagines the possibility of a mother killing her own children. In the *Letter to d'Alembert*

Rousseau cites Euripides' *Medea* as the classic example. Jealous hatred of her husband Jason causes her to break the bonds of nature.

If birth is to be a sacred relation that forms a bond between mother and child, then intercourse must be sanctified. The child cannot be separated from its origins if birth is a determinative act. This means that it is the duty of a mother to ensure that her child has a father, and Rousseau states this as the first duty of the female from which all others flow. If a child is to have a father then marriage must be sacred. Julie's law against adultery founds the rights of fathers on the instincts of mothers. Rousseau's romantic credo finds a maternal foundation for marriage and family.

Julie's inability to abandon all for love is in striking contrast to St. Preux. He is so free from other attachments that we do not even know his name. He is only Julie's lover. His parents are dead. He has sold what little property he had inherited, and he cannot even be called a citizen in the narrowest sense of the term. His freedom is reflected in his study of men and their manners. He is interested in the best form of human association—whether it is better to live in the remotest village or the most populated city, rather than the particular association he was born into. Julie, on the other hand, is not concerned about the best form of association. She resigns herself to the laws under which she was born because she is grateful to them for her life and the things she loves. She could abandon her fondest hope of love before she could abandon the laws.

The opposition between St. Preux and Julie on the question of birth is a reflection on gender. Rousseau chose to make the male lover rootless, and the female surrounded by friends and family. The differences between St. Preux and Julie are reflected in the different educations of Emile and Sophie.[33] Rousseau recognizes a social necessity stemming from the different bodies of male and female. Julie could not abandon her father, and she affirmed the primacy of birth because she was thinking of her own children. The first lesson taught to Sophie is that life is a lineage of dead mothers who are survived by their daughters.[34] Rousseau attempts to build upon the most basic maternal instinct.

The male does not have the same immediate attachment to a child as does the female. The male is attached to his children through imagination more than through an immediate feeling. For St. Preux, children would only be a doubling of his love; he can only think of them in romantic terms. Wolmar thinks of his children in their maturation. Julie's immediate instincts and Wolmar's more distant attachment is reflected in the places they occupy with respect to the education of their boys. Julie will educate them until the dawn of reason, then Wolmar and St. Preux will take over. Wolmar loves them, but he cannot occupy himself with them in their pre-rational condition. Julie is capable of the connections that depend more on imagination, but they are secondary to her immediate love of her children as her own.

The importance of reproduction to female sexuality is also seen in Claire. Claire is Julie's friend and confidante, just as Bomston is St. Preux's friend and confidant. Claire, like Bomston, is inclined more to friendship than either love, marriage, or family. But, she, unlike Bomston, does not remain unmarried and childless. Claire's husband dies and she gives her daughter to Julie to educate. She returns to being a friend, but that friendship is enhanced through their children. Rousseau argues that the perfection of a man is less connected with his gender than the perfection of a woman. [35] Rousseau is very hard on unmarried women. They are either servants to other women and their children, or they are prostitutes.

Claire's friendship with Julie is a reform of the friendship between Miss Howe and Clarissa. Virtue alone united them. Miss Howe is a spirited admirer and defender of Clarissa. Like Claire, Miss Howe gets a simple, but decent, man for a husband. And just as Claire forces M. d'Orbe to assist in a plan to save Julie's reputation before marrying him, Miss Howe forces Mr. Hickman to help Clarissa. The spirited Claire and Miss Howe are united to their husbands less from love and admiration for them than from gratitude for their assistance to their respective friends.

Yet, the friendship between Miss Howe and Clarissa is never made tender through love and family, whereas Claire helps Julie and St. Preux, and gives her own child to Julie. Harriet does not divide them, but brings them closer together. Neither Miss Howe nor Clarissa have children, nor are either married (Miss Howe will marry Hickman after the action of the novel). The tenderness between Miss Howe and Clarissa depends more upon suffering and pity than love. We do not even see them together. Julie and Claire, on the other hand, are called the inseparables. They are blood cousins who have known one another since birth.

Miss Howe vows vengeance against Clarissa's persecutors after her death, whereas Claire makes a curse against anyone who shall disturb Julie. The death of Lovelace and the calamities, which befall the Harlowe family, will undoubtedly give Miss Howe satisfaction. Claire needs to be reunited with Julie and she does so through Harriet. Love and family enhances the friendship between them.

Julie is the link between the two halves of *La Nouvelle Héloïse* because the dual aspects of sex are, by nature, more inherent to her than to men. This duality, no doubt, divides her life, but it also enables her to rule through her beauty and to be the foundation and centerpiece of what Rousseau believes to be an example of one of the highest forms of civilization.

No one picked up and understood the importance of women to modern man more than Tocqueville. In *Democracy in America*, he writes,

> if anyone asks me what I think the chief cause of the extraordinary prosperity and growing power of this nation, I should answer that it is due to the superiority of their women. [36]

He understands the superiority of American women in comparison to European women. The comparison is part of his more general theme: aristocracy versus democracy. He argues that although American women have more freedom than their aristocratic counterparts, they are, nonetheless, not given to libertinism, and that their choices are not unregulated by judgement about virtue and compatibility. In an aristocracy, the freedom of the heart has a bad reputation because love is pernicious to its institutions and its institutions are pernicious to love. A suitor who disregards the conventions is likely to be of questionable character, and a woman who cannot legitimate her love in the eyes of the public is not likely to think carefully about the constancy and virtue of her lover. In a liberal democracy, however, a woman's choice is the basis for her marriage and is, therefore, not a thing to be taken lightly. The freedom of the American woman, of which Tocqueville writes, is not the freedom to choose a lover or a career, but the freedom to choose a husband. The romantic imagination flies very close to the ground in America, and his remarks about the early maturity of the American female, and her good sense and judgement, remind one of the description of the young Genevan females. Woman's freedom is exercised within the limits of her sex; her pride is to accept her duties and stand by her choice.[37] Tocqueville, like Rousseau, argues that the freedom of women ought to be exercised within the limits of modesty and domesticity:

> In Europe, there are people who, confusing the divergent attributes of the sexes, claim to make, of a man and a woman, creatures, who are, not equal only, but actually similar. They would attribute the same functions to both, impose the same duties and grant the same rights; they would have them share everything—work, pleasure, public affairs. It is easy to see that the sort of equality forced on both sexes degrades them both, and that so coarse a jumble of nature's works could produce nothing but feeble men and unseemly women.[38]

Tocqueville's admiration for American women is part of his Rousseauian solution to Rousseauian problems. Tocqueville is convinced of the justice of democracy, and he foresees its complete victory over aristocracy. Like Rousseau, he is a supporter of freedom and equality, and, like Rousseau, is concerned with establishing a choiceworthy life on those ideas. Tocqueville is less concerned with the tyranny of persecution than with a new form of tyranny unique to modern democracies. He characterizes modern tyranny as one of conformism and of materialism.[39] Equality and American political institutions foster the rule of public opinion. The spirit of the individual is crushed when faced with a consensus monster that drowns out the sound of one's own voice. Furthermore, the love of equality fosters conformism because one does not mind being on a leash as long as society holds the end of it rather than a superior.

The counterpart to the conformist public mind is the material private life. The almost impossibility of grand politics throws the individual back on himself where his existence threatens to be consumed by sensual pleasures and material pursuits. Tocqueville must make suggestions for how to keep the understanding from being swallowed up by abstract, general, and mass causes, and how to keep pleasures and ambitions from being degraded by the material.

This is, of course, the character of Parisian despotism—enslavement to public opinion, which is neither reason, nor belief, and enslavement to the preservation and sensations of the body. Like Rousseau, Tocqueville sees modern man threatened by the abyss outside of himself and the abyss within himself. Conformism and materialism are his self-willed blinders, which he does not dare take off, but which he cannot help but glimpse through.

Even Tocqueville's suggestions and solutions are taken from the pages of La Nouvelle Héloïse. He attempts to preserve humanity by preserving the awareness of virtue in its various aspects. History, literature, the fine arts, religion, and philosophy are for Tocqueville (as they are for Rousseau) ways of preserving the awareness of the beautiful and, therewith, an understanding of man that can comprehend the divine in him. The beautiful can only be perceived with the assistance of the imagination, and Tocqueville, like Rousseau, tries to turn the eyes upward. His discussion of the difference between modern democratic and ancient history is taken from St. Preux's discussion of ancient and modern history.[40] Like St. Preux, he recommends the study of the ancients because, in ancient times, men were less constricted by institutions; they could act more freely as individuals and could cause great effects. One can learn about morals from the ancients because one can see men acting and deliberating. The moderns see abstract and determinative causes to the extent that they lose sight of their own freedom. The problems of literature, the fine arts, religion, and philosophy are similar and have similar solutions—the study of the ancients. The ancients correct the defects of conformism and materialism because they have as their subjects, greatness and immortality, rather than the familiar and useful.

Tocqueville, like Rousseau, is a curious example of a democratic thinker who returns to the ancients with the exception of an unclassical elevation of the female. The ancients may correct the worst tendencies of the democratic mind, but the female is responsible for the morals of the country. The democratic family is the one element of American democracy that Tocqueville finds touching, and in which he sees a naturalness that is not coarse. He is part of the romantic movement, in so far as he looks to the family and women as modern man's one chance to avoid the Scylla and Charybdis of conformism and materialism. The democratic family promises to provide a real sentiment that accompanies morality and God, and is, therefore, neither aristocratic in its authority nor democratic in its individualism.

There is no book that informs Tocqueville's *Democracy in America* more than *La Nouvelle Héloïse*. But, Rousseau did not dream of preserving the taste and mind that is the flower of aristocracy in a liberal democracy. While it is true that his romanticism undercuts class distinctions, and his portrait of familial sentiments undercut patriarchal authority, it is, nonetheless, the case that his portrait of the society at Clarens is an assimilation of the aristocracy into private life, not into a democracy with a ruling principle of equality. The charm of Clarens owes much to the fruits of aristocracy.

The overcoming of class finds its greatest expression in love and friendship. They are the relations that reveal a real concern for the true, the good, and the beautiful. In the first part of the novel we saw friendship formed around love, only to find love unsuccessful in its attempt to live free of convention. In the second half of the novel, friendship has a more independent meaning, but is still subordinate; it is informed by the concerns of family. Friendship is not given to passionate hope and is, therefore, more in harmony with the temperament of marriage and family, even though it does not share its end. The friendship between Wolmar, Bomston, and St. Preux is an example of humanity stretching over the lines of class. Their temperaments suit their different classes, as well as their different minds. The rational Wolmar was born a prince; the spirited Bomston, a noble; and the passionate St. Preux, a commoner. Their friendship is not easily solidified because of St. Preux's manifest inequality with respect to wealth, birth, and experience. Friendship is not a relation of superior and inferior, but a relation between equals. Wolmar and Bomston must suffer from defects that make them need St. Preux. The necessary weaknesses are found in Bomston's sexual desire and Wolmar's inability to face mortality. Bomston's spiritedness and Stoic philosophy leave him helpless in the face of his desires, and Wolmar's reason cannot digest the necessity of death. Rousseau's portrait of a community without the barriers of class is not founded on the abstract idea of equality, but on the partiality of existence and the need for wholeness through virtue. The friends must be both teacher and student to one another.

Once Julie is married, St. Preux must learn to live without the hope of possessing her. He was a slave to his love. After Julie renounces him, he withers into a state of despair that is moderated by self-pity.[41] He reasons about suicide in order to be talked out of it by Bomston. His friendship with Bomston preserves his heart; he is grateful to Bomston and can, therefore, find a reason to continue his life—to pay his debt of gratitude to his friend. Bomston sends him on a voyage where he will either learn to live with his pain and disappointment, or die. The Stoic teaches the Platonist that an unhappy love is an instrument of education, not by teaching equanimity of mind, but by teaching one to struggle with the pain hoisted on one by fortune and the passions.

The futility of Bomston's philosophy is revealed in his own case. He is no match for his passions. He falls in love with a reformed prostitute and plans to bring her to Clarens to live amongst Julie and Claire.[42] The marriage cannot bring happiness since Laura would have to suffer the company of virtuous women, and since she could not but dishonor Bomston. St. Preux (the Platonist) teaches Bomston to sacrifice the consummation of his love in order to preserve its ideal.[43] Laura enters a convent and Bomston vows never to marry another woman. The Stoic teaches the Platonist to endure the vagaries of another's will, while the Platonist teaches the Stoic to preserve his love by sacrificing the enjoyment of it.

Whereas Bomston helped St. Preux learn to live with the pains of his love, Wolmar (the Epicurean) promises to make him happy by curing him of his love. Wolmar hopes to cure him by presenting to him a Julie, who is no longer his lover, but his friend's wife and the mother of his friend's children. Seeing her in light of these other relations is supposed to extinguish the possibility and hope of his love by extinguishing its object. Wolmar wants St. Preux's heart to take refuge in the past. The hope is that he can love Julie under two different aspects, that he can indulge his memory of her as a girl without wanting to possess her as a wife and mother.

Wolmar's cure for St. Preux is a consequence of his materialism. He tries to manipulate sense impressions in order to drive out certain passions and develop new ones. His materialism does not, however, provide him with a solution to death. He wants St. Preux to be like a brother to Julie because he wants St. Preux to live with her in order to educate his children. Wolmar is too old to educate his sons. He needs a friend who will love his children as his own, who is also educated and who will not seduce his wife. Wolmar lives in relation to an image of continuity through his children. St. Preux helps him preserve these hopes. St. Preux will also assist in converting Wolmar to the belief in the existence of God. The death of Julie brings Wolmar's education of St. Preux to an end and allows St. Preux to become Wolmar's teacher.

Rousseau does not recognize in friendship an autonomous end that can claim independence from love and family. The friendship, between the baron and Wolmar, was a friendship between military men that was subservient to war (Wolmar saved the baron's life), but was also based on their compatibility. Yet, their friendship is subordinated to family by the baron's need for an heir and Wolmar's need for a tender attachment. The friendship between these two men is in sharp contrast to Aristotle's treatment of friendship. Aristotle argues that, since peace is the end of war, friendship must find its highest expression in leisure, which is the end of peace. Aristotle has very great difficulty portraying a friendship between morally virtuous and self-sufficient men at leisure. He even finds it diffi-

cult to explain how they could need one another, as they are self-sufficient. But, Aristotle never suggests that friendship is subordinate to reproduction and marriage, nor does he subject friendship to love interests
as is the case with Bomston and St. Preux. Rousseau bounds friendship
by the sexual and reproductive organs, whereas Aristotle stretches his
understanding of friendship toward the unity of the mind. The community established at the end of the novel owes everything to Julie. Its members' interest in her gives them a lasting interest in one another. The
heroic Bomston has a tender admiration for her; the baron continues his
name through her; the detached Wolmar forms a tender attachment
through her, and St. Preux lives for her. Nothing could be more unclassical than the sovereignty of this extraordinary female.

Julie's sovereignty is seen in her victories over the old order. She is
responsible for bending the knee of both Bomston and the baron. The
bending of their knees make way for love and family, respectively. As
Bomston and the baron were preeminent in the old order, St. Preux and
Wolmar are in the new ones. Julie will be at the core of these new orders
as she was at the reform of the old ones.

NOTES

1. *Letter to d'Alembert*, p. 82.
2. *La Nouvelle Héloïse*, III, xviii, p. 340.
3. Rousseau often had to answer the paradox of being a novelist and playwright
who spoke against the arts. He answers the paradox in several places, but nowhere as
thematically and extensively as in the preface to *Narcisse*. His formula is that entertainments are bad for good people, and good for bad people.
4. Lovelace is clearly one of literature's Don Juans. He is not, however, a Don Juan
tailored for the tastes of polite society. Stendhal says that Molière's Don Juan is a good
companion, who wants to be admired at the court of a galant and spiritual, young
king (*Chroniques italiennes* [Gallimard, 1952] p. 48). Molière's Don Juan is torn between
his pleasures and his nobility. In order to enjoy his taste for variety, he must lie to
others about who he is. He goes to hell because he is unwilling to acknowledge his
baseness and sins. The mix of pride and hedonism characteristic of a real Don Juan
results in brutality because his sensuality is a spirited rebellion against Christianity
and the church. The general theme of the conflict between spirited rebellion against
the law with its justification in the goodness of pleasure has its classic treatment in
Socrates' discussions with Polus and Callicles in the *Gorgias*.
5. Stendhal, *On Love*, trans. Sale (Bungay, 1984), pp. 28, 90.
6. Stendhal, *Life of Rossini*, trans. Calder (New York, 1985), p. 468.
7. Samuel Richardson, *Clarissa*, ed. Ross (London, 1988), p. 1498.
8. *La Nouvelle Héloïse*, II, iii, p. 197.
9. Ibid., Vi, xiii, p. 745.
10. Ibid., I, lx, p. 165. Compare this with the character of Clarissa and what Richardson said about it himself: "In a word, if in the history before us, it shall be found that
the spirit is duly diffused throughout, that the characters are various and natural, well
distinguished, and uniformly supported and maintained: *if there be a variety of incidents
sufficient to excite attention, and those so conducted to keep the reader always awake*, the
length, then, must add proportionally to the pleasure that every person of taste receives from a well-drawn picture of nature. But, where the contrary of all these qual-

ities shock the understanding, the extravagant performance will be judged tedious, though no longer than a fairy tale." (Postscript to *Clarissa*, italics are mine.)

11. *La Nouvelle Héloïse*, I, i, p. 32 and III, xviii, p. 340.

12. Ibid., I, xii, pp. 59, 60.

13. *Letter to d'Alembert*, p. 33.

14. *La Nouvelle Héloïse*, III, xiv, p. 332.

15. The translation is from Rousseau's French translation found in the Duchesne-Coindet. The quote itself is from *The Life and Death of Laura*, Sonnet cccxxxviii.

16. Ibid., I, lvii, p. 152.

17. Ibid., p. 159.

18. Ibid., p. 160.

19. Ibid., III, xxii, p. 391.

20. Plato, *Apology of Socrates*, ed. Burnet (Oxford, 1986), l. 20a5.

21. *La Nouvelle Heloise*, I, lx, p. 163.

22. Ibid., p. 164.

23. Plato, *Republic*, trans. Bloom (New York, 1968), l.335d4.

24. Ibid., p. 165.

25. Friedrich Nietzsche, *Beyond Good and Evil*, trans. Kaufmann, (New York, 1966), p. 259.

26. *La Nouvelle Héloïse*, I, lxii, p. 169.

27. *Beyond Good and Evil*, pp. 238–39.

28. *Emile*, p. 357.

29. In the *Second Discourse*, Rousseau distinguishes physical love from moral love. He also distinguishes the cry from physical pain from the crying at death, which is connected to belief in God or gods.

30. Jean-Jacques Rousseau, *On The Social Contract*, trans. Masters, (New York, 1978), p. 131.

31. *La Nouvelle Héloïse*, III, xviii, pp. 359–63.

32. Ibid., III, xviii, p. 363.

33. *Emile*, p. 357.

34. Ibid., pp. 379, 380.

35. Ibid., p. 358.

36. Alexis de Tocqueville, *Democracy in America*, trans. Lawrence, (New York, 1969), p. 603

37. Ibid., p. 602.

38. Ibid., pp. 600, 601.

39. Ibid., pp. 690–702.

40. Ibid., pp. 493–96. St. Preux's letter on history is found in I, xii, p. 60.

41. *La Nouvelle Héloïse*, III, xxi.

42. The details of Bomston's affair in Italy are contained in an appendix to *La Nouvelle Héloïse* entitled "Les Amours de Milord Edouard Bomston." As in Paris, the leading female roles in Rome are played by a marquess and a prostitute. But, in Rome, there is passionate love, rather than indifference and dissoluteness. The marquess is insanely jealous of Bomston's love for Laura, Bomston kills the marquise in a duel, and Laura suffers the shame of her trade. Bomston's love affairs in Rome are never consummated. He will not commit adultery with the marquess, and Laura will not allow herself to be touched by him; she cannot even endure the possibility that he might treat her like a public woman. The pleasures of Rome are not the carnal ones. Bomston enjoys his victories over his passions; the marquess seeks to satisfy the vindictiveness of her jealousy; and, Laura is exalted by her reawakened heart and the thought of being loved by a man of passion and virtue. In Rome, the spiritual dominates nature, but its dominion is not treated by Rousseau as it is by Petrarch. Rousseau treats the chastity of his Laura as the redemption of a fallen woman, rather than as the virtue of the female, and his depiction of the divine is in its jealous anger. In Rome, one finds the striking effects of the depths and the heights, which Rousseau kept out of the main body.

43. Rousseau follows De Lorris' famous medieval poem *Le Roman de la Rose* in making the friends confidants in the affairs of love.

THREE

Rousseau's Romantic Alternatives

Love and Family

Love and family are alternatives to the pedestrian chaos of enlightened Paris and the paternal authority of Vevey. They are attempts to form meaningful connections on the basis of the sensual pleasure of intercourse and the continuity of procreation, respectively. They moderate the indifference of science and the authority of Christian patriarchy. This moderation is seen in Rousseau's synthesis between intercourse, procreation, ancient philosophy, and Christianity. Reason and God are harmonized on the strengths of erotic and procreative attachments.

Rousseau's portrayal of love and family as a way of moderating reason and belief has as its model Prévost's *Le Philosophe Anglais ou Histoire de Monsieur Cleveland*. Cleveland is the bastard son of Cromwell. He is outside of the law in birth, as well as in habit. He is raised in a cave where he is taught ancient philosophy rather than Christianity. From Plato, he has learned about the divine; from Seneca, he has learned self-control; and, from the Epicureans, he has learned about pleasure. The story of his life, like that of Wolmar, is about his conversion to God. He comes to believe in the immortality of individual souls. His conversion is a consequence of his love for his daughter Cecile. He thought she was murdered shortly after birth, only to discover her fifteen years later. He fell in love with her and was going to marry her before learning their true relation. Not long after their reunion, Cecile dies from an oppressed heart. Unable to give expression to her love for her father, she cannot even console her suffering with complaints. Her heart cannot even hope to legitimize itself; she gladly dies because she knows her situation is hopeless.

The death of Cecile converts Cleveland. Plato's impersonal divinity is of no support; Stoic courage cannot dry his tears; and, Epicurean happi-

ness cannot make him forget. Her death is insupportable and reveals to
him the existence of God.

The greatest difference between *La Nouvelle Héloïse* and *Cleveland* is
that Rousseau's novel gets its unity from a female rather than a male.
Rousseau divides the philosophic traits of Cleveland into three different
characters, and instead of connecting three or four women around the
male, as does Prévost, Rousseau connects three or four men to his Julie.
Although Prévost is sympathetic to love and family, he treats them merely as connections that prepare belief. The theme of natural religion versus
Christianity is in the forefront, to the extent that love of a female is never
divinized, and family life is never considered heaven on earth. In *La
Nouvelle Héloïse*, God supports these relations more than they support
Him. It is revealing that the death of a daughter converts Cleveland,
whereas the death of a wife converts Wolmar. One expects to be separated from a daughter, but not a wife. Wolmar does not merely believe that
Julie lives and is in safe hands, but that she is with him.

The female is the center of Rousseau's novel because the body is the
center of Rousseau's thought. Reason and God are derivative. Intercourse
and procreation are the aspects of body best suited to linking it to a
community with a common good and a shared destiny because the sexual and procreative organs are a point of contact with others and because
they are connected to the imagination more than other parts of the body.
Nature, reason, and God are parts of the whole, which divide man and
whose unity poses a problem. We must examine love and family under
the aspects of nature, reason, and God if we are to understand *La Nouvelle
Héloïse*.

La Nouvelle Héloïse begins with a confession of love from a twenty-
year-old boy to an eighteen-year-old girl. It is a classic case of love at first
sight. He has been tutoring her for ten months, and, although they have
kept silent, their hearts have understood something of each other's. But
he must finally speak because he finds his condition intolerable. He
wishes to be cured of his love, or, to die. The fate of his passion must be
decided one way or another. He must take steps toward relieving himself
of his pain, though he cannot cure it himself. He must solicit Julie's will.
The solicitation gives him some relief, but it is hardly a cure. The first
cure he proposes is to have Julie banish him. Yet, shortly after asking to
be banished, he proposes another cure for his torment: he asks Julie to be
more reserved during their child-like games in order to torment him less.
He, therefore, asks to be both banished and to remain. The contradictions
of his first letter express the confusion of love's first steps.

Everything suggests that his request to be banished is not sincere,
although he is aware that leaving would be the decent and prudent thing
to do. That he thinks leaving would be the decent thing to do is evident
by his weak attempt to justify his remaining with reasons of propriety.
He says it would be improper to leave without an explanation after Ju-

lie's mother was so good as to invite him into her home. Would it be more decent to corrupt her only daughter? That he thinks his love is imprudent is evident by his hoping against his reason. He says that the ardor of his passion encourages him and even presents him illusions of destiny, whereas his reason disavows hope. Is it not imprudent for a poor bourgeois to seek the hand of a baron's daughter? His request to be banished is a proposal that attenuates his offense to decency and to prudence. Propriety and prudence are easily silenced by love. Their weakness suggests that there are more powerful reasons for his proposal of banishment. Certainly, he does not want to offend Julie's modesty with his boldness, and, fearing the worst, he does not want to get his hopes up too high.

Even though he is cautious, he attempts to justify himself. He says that he respects her noble birth and charms. Yet, birth and charms would be nothing without her virtue. He believes he has found a beauty of soul that is the true ground for human relations. What meaning can money, title, and beauty of body have, compared to virtue? He believes that his passion is justified, that it is not criminal because he loves what is best and lasting about Julie. He believes that his heart understands her, and that she might even learn what she is through his heart.

Accompanying the justification of his passion is the hope to remain with Julie. He asks her to change her behavior in order to alleviate his torment. He hopes that she will sympathize with his torment. He even hopes that she will love him in return, for he chastises her for not behaving more like a woman in love; she should be cold in public and tender in private rather than the opposite. St. Preux's confession of love is, thus, part confession, part justification, and part prayer. He cannot feel guilty about his passion, but he respects it and Julie enough to be cautious in fulfilling it.

In the second letter, we learn that neither of his solutions has worked. Julie did not banish him, and her change of behavior has only increased his torment. She is no longer playful in public, and, in private, she is even more severe. In the first letter, St. Preux still held to some hope of conquering his passion without satisfying it. In the second letter, it is clear that he is past indifference, and that no precautions are going to cure him of his love. Her severity in private (which he takes for her displeasure) brings home to him how much he sought to have his love reciprocated. Her displeasure forces him to reflect on hatred and contempt. He says that he could better tolerate hatred of his passion than contempt for it because the former is directed at his crime while the latter is directed at his person. He cannot endure being despised by the one he loves. Furthermore, hatred of a crime is not cut off from pity as much as is contempt. Hatred can be satisfied by punishment and, thereby, attend upon a hope for reconciliation. He, therefore, tells her that she would pity him if she knew how much pain she was giving him and that the criminal is no longer hated once he is dead. The language of crime and punishment is music to his ears compared to disdain. But contempt is worse than hatred not only because it is more personal and less hopeful, but also because it is more unjust. He believes that his passion is good, and that while it might pose certain dangers, it is too pure and promising to deserve contempt.

The third letter completes his suffering. Here, we find him with the strength to decide his own fate. He is now prepared to banish himself. He has neither conquered his passion with reason, nor subjected it to decency; he says that he is sacrificing his passion. His passion has disturbed Julie's tranquillity, and so, in order to restore her to her natural cheerfulness, he has decided to leave. He does not think of his self-banishment as a defeat, but, rather, as a triumph of love. Love never comes into itself until it makes sacrifices for the beloved. The lover claims to live for the beloved and, hence, can feel the sincerity of his attachment only when making a sacrifice. His suffering is dearer to him than his happiness, or, even his life, for, although his sacrifices are painful, they do not destroy the character of his attachment to the beloved. If he has to choose between degrading his love in order to succeed (putting his desires before her happiness) or sacrificing his desire, he would rather endure the suffering of a sacrifice, for, at least, he would maintain the feelings that are the meaning of his life. His greatest fear is to degrade himself or his beloved, thereby destroying love's ideals and causing a state of indifference.

But St. Preux's sacrifice is not simply a way of preserving his attachment by preserving its noble character. By characterizing his banishment to her as a sacrifice, he reveals that he does not simply want to restore her to her tranquillity. He does not want to behold her from afar, as one does the beauty of the stars. She is unlike the stars in that she has a will and is capable of recognizing him. St. Preux hopes that Julie will recognize his sacrifice, that she will learn to respect his passion, and regret having shown contempt for it by not responding to his letters. He is even a little hopeful that she will ask him to remain, for he criticizes her treatment of him while promising to leave. Why criticize at a moment of separation if not to illicit a hoped-for response? Perhaps sacrifices are always accompanied by hope.

The first three letters are clearly a genealogy of love. St. Preux says as much and catalogues the stages. At first, he thought his passion could be conquered in time with his reason. Next, he felt the torment of displeasing the one he loves. And finally, he felt the pain of disturbing the tranquillity of the one he loves. The genealogy deserves some reflection because its elements will reappear throughout the novel.

In the first stage, he spoke of prudence. Although it was clear that passion had the upper hand, he struggled with it in an attempt to retain his sanity. He sought to limit his passion by the possible. He tried to cure his passion without flattering it and indulging it. Conquering one's passion through reason is notoriously stoic. Certainly, Rousseau identifies the conquest of passion through reason most with Seneca the Stoic. And Bomston, the Stoic in the novel, says that he arrived at reason by route of the passions. The most famous trait of the Stoic is the attempt to conquer the pains of fortune in order to be the sole source of his own happiness. The Stoic looks at life as the attempt to overcome suffering for the sake of self-sufficient happiness. In order to achieve this God-like independence, he must free himself from attachments, for, if he were attached to things that are subject to chance (even his own body), he would be subject to the vagaries of life. The Stoic, thus understood, is an extreme example of reason conquering the passions. He must use his reason to cultivate a state of indifference. One can attempt to cultivate a state of indifference by destroying the hopes that fuel passion. All passion that is not immediate bodily appetite requires the hope of satisfying itself in order to be sustained. If reason were to destroy the hopes of love, it would effectively destroy love. But could a young man in love for the first time possibly see the problems of love? It is not surprising that reason has little hold on him.

In the second letter, we see St. Preux in his weakest and most pitiful condition. Far from being a Stoic, we find him at the mercy of Julie because he is at the mercy of his passion for her. He is without resource other than begging. His reason is of no effect. He cannot deny that, more than anything else, he wants his love reciprocated. In the second letter, he reminds us of Wolmar, the Epicurean, who is overwhelmed by the need to satisfy his love for Julie. Wolmar's reason has very little force over his passions. Reason is a passive beholder for Wolmar; he loves order and observation. When he finally does feel a passion, he is unable to resist it. He stands opposite the Stoic, whose reason is defined by struggle with the passions. We must wonder if there is a way to combine passion and reason, attachment and detachment, in a harmonious way. Is there a mean between the Epicurean and the Stoic?

In the third letter, St. Preux deifies his beloved and his love. He regrets having disturbed her tranquillity with his passion. He promises to sacrifice the satisfaction of his passion and to serve love only by worshipping Julie. The purification of his passion relieves him from the torment of his passion. He is relieved because he has consolations for his sacrifice. He proves himself to be worthy of loving and being loved. He transcends fortune's rejection by proving himself deserving to be happy. And he even hopes in some way to be rewarded for his desert. He emerges from his unhappy love in neither a state of indifference, nor a state of despair, but a state of defiant and expectant piety. He wants to be worthy of the happiness he has been denied and hopes that, somewhere and somehow, his worthiness will be recognized and, perhaps, rewarded. One could say that he sublimates his passion by finding in his beloved the promise of satisfactions rather than the satisfactions themselves and by proving himself to be worthy of happiness rather than being happy. He neither frees himself from his passion nor satisfies it. He maintains his attachment without becoming completely dependent upon the will of the beloved. This combination of attachment and detachment, achieved through the deification of love, reminds us of Plato (the philosopher, who is recognized as St. Preux's teacher).[1] Plato is presented as a mean between the Epicurean and the Stoic. The stages of St. Preux's love are clearly related to the three ancient schools. Stoicism, Epicureanism, and Platonism are meant to reveal something of the character of reason, nature, and the divine, respectively. In these first letters, Rousseau gives us a glimpse of the whole.

The three stages of love, and their corresponding characters and philosophies, are suited to the three different aspects of private life—friendship, family, and love. A Stoic is more suited to being a friend first and foremost than the other two. Friendship does not require (it even precludes) intercourse and a concern with physical beauty. Spiritedness is good for friendship because it requires devotion where there is no physical pleasure; one does not possess a friend as one possesses a beloved or a spouse. Friendship is more evidently directed toward shared virtue than either love and family. It is better characterized by mutual admiration than mutual possession.

The Epicurean is best suited for marriage and family because they are characterized by tranquillity. Marriage and family are less personal than friendship and love. Husband and wife do not live to be with one another. They are the most important parts of the household and they are the cornerstone of society. They must please one another, but the mad passion of love and the devotion of a friend would only make them lose the taste for their duties and the serenity accompanying their togetherness.

The Platonist is best suited for love because he can sustain the character of passionate attachment through the belief in a separate world. Platonic idealism complements love because love is threatened by the satisfaction of the senses and by familiarity. Love is meant to be forever. If it is to preserve the character of the attachment that is its meaning, then lovers must not become husband and wife; they must sacrifice their longing to be together with one another exclusively forever if they are to preserve their love. The separations that take place between Julie and St. Preux are not simply meant to show the obstacles that love encounters. The separations are like the separations of the rivulet at Clarens. One small rivulet is separated and reunited by the gardener so that from this weak source is created an oasis given the name of *Elysium*. Sublimation is the art of taking the sexual desire, that is, in and of itself, nothing, and attaching it to an object of love, hope, and devotion. If one wants to understand the meaning of sublimation, one must not only learn to feel with love, but also one must trace the course it must travel in order to preserve its meaning. The love of Julie and St. Preux is united, separated, and sent underground, only to emerge as a truth expressed in terms of a romantic hope in the afterlife.

It turns out that St. Preux has misunderstood Julie. He took her silence and discomposure for severity and contempt. But, in fact, she was only fearful of love's first connection. She, too, fell in love at first sight. But she is even less taken with his outer appearance and gallantry than he was with her birth and charms. She longs for an eternal attachment and is, therefore, touched by a man of probity, rather than fashion. Her fear is easily understandable since she must be careful not to be fooled. What is harder to understand are the insults she hurls upon St. Preux. She calls him a vile seducer and hates him for wrenching a confession of love from her. She is indignant because she believes that she is ruined, that the first step is the one onto the precipice of dishonor.

But her love is far greater than her fear and indignation. She cannot conquer the poison that runs through her veins. But, unlike St. Preux, she did not turn to reason in her first attempts to conquer her passion; she looked to God. But God gave her no more strength than did reason for St. Preux. God and reason prove to be ineffective restraints on love. St. Preux cannot disavow his expectations for supreme happiness, and Julie cannot hate herself for inspiring such longings. She, like St. Preux, wants to be cured of her love, or die. Love's pains are unendurable without the hope of relief. They are not like pains of the body that can be endured for the sake of living. The satisfactions of love are the meaning of life, and, hence, death is to be preferred to a life without love.

Julie does not really believe that love will ruin her, and, thus, she seeks a way to preserve both her honor and her love. One possibility is to play the coquette in order to be obeyed. The coquette attempts to maintain her honor and her attachment by promising satisfactions, which she has no intention of fulfilling. Julie rejects coquetry as a despicable art that is inconsistent with the honesty of love. Furthermore, she thinks she would be better protected by admitting the danger and enlisting her enemy as her ally. Unable to trust her own strength, she relies on St. Preux's respect for her virtue and his self-restraint. She says that, if he were cowardly enough to abuse her trust, then, her contempt for him would cure her of her passion. She loves both virtue and St. Preux. She would regret the loss of her virtue as much as she would regret to discover him a coward.

Both Julie and St. Preux think that virtue and love are not in absolute contradiction with one another. The respect lovers feel toward one another and themselves is similar to virtue. Love is a source of respect that is threatened by the senses. What would Julie and St. Preux be in themselves and to one another if they just satisfied their senses as they would their hunger or their thirst? How would they differ from the animals?

The self-understanding of the lover is not that of a scientist nor that of a hedonist. St. Preux believes that his love is so generous and chaste that Julie's doubts degrade it and insult it. Love is similar to virtue in that it raises man above his immediate sensations. It differs from virtue in that it has a physical aspect that is clearly directed toward pleasure.

Not content to trust her own strength and St. Preux's strength, Julie asks her friend Claire to help protect her from herself. This request is the perfect vehicle for testing the friendship between them, because, as Claire argues, jealousy destroys most friendships between women. Claire is enlisted as a defender of Julie's honor, who will do all she can do consistent with friendship to protect that honor.

At the end of Letter VI, there is an intentional lacuna that marks the end of the section. The major conflicts have been established. Julie loves both virtue and St. Preux, and she seems to have found a solution to satisfy the demands of both.

The second section begins with a lover's complaint. St. Preux knows that he ought to be happy, but he is not. He is not willing to call virtue an illusion, but he makes it clear that suffering virtue's restraints needs some kind of compensation. Without compensation, virtue seems unjust. He feels that an injustice is being done to him, because, while he suffers and languishes, Julie is recovering her health. The injustice he feels is not that love is onerous to him and beneficial to her; her health suggests to him that she is not grateful, that she, for whom he suffers, does not acknowledge his pains. Her esteem for him is the only compensation he can imagine for a life of restraint. He thinks that she does not acknowledge his sacrifices because his experience of passion is one of suffering, and, conversely, he believes that her spriteliness is an effect of a superficial attachment; he believes that her spriteliness is capriciousness. She justifies her health as the effect of joy. She has discovered to her relief that the pleasure of being loved can exist side by side with honor. She communicates her joy to St. Preux, who finds that she is not capricious, but, like the angels, is above passion. The beauty of her joy soothes his passion. Yet, he cannot but believe that supreme happiness requires a union of both body and soul, that supreme happiness must be supremely pleasurable, not under the constraint of virtue.

In letter XI, we see Julie's recognition of St. Preux's sufferings. He has kept his word and has successfully preserved the treasure entrusted to him. She knows that he respects her virtue, that he was not feigning respect in order to take his pleasures. She believes that he could not enjoy his pleasure at her expense. She now begins to pity his suffering (and hopes to relieve him from it) now that she believes he is not a seducer. St. Preux has undergone a test, which he has passed. The test of respect is not simply a convention used to repress desire, or to give women control of male sexual desire; the test is necessary for the flowering of love. His proofs are what convince her that their destinies are inextricably bound together. And, as she makes clear, there is no touching of souls without the belief in shared happiness. The possibility of separation is separation in fact, that is why love depends on the belief in a shared destiny. There can be no shared destiny, however, if there is no common good. Self-protection, pleasure, and reputation cannot alone form a common good. Female modesty, and the respect for it, accompany an awareness and an assurance that the natural attraction between a man and a woman is exclusive, eternal, and the supreme good for both.

Love is more than a permanent attachment. Julie believes that her attachments to her parents and to Claire are permanent, but she does not experience true being in relation to them. Her existence as a daughter and as a friend has an element of the conditional. Her parents do not love her for herself, but as their own. Claire loves her for herself, but their friendship precludes bodily union and pleasure. Friendship does not promise a complete bodily and spiritual satisfaction because it is not consummated in intercourse. Love is more passionate than friendship. It is full of sufferings and hopes, which are alien to friendship because it promises to be much more than friendship. Friendship requires a shared activity and cannot, therefore, promise to be the end of life. The permanence of the attachment between Julie and St. Preux does not require that they be always together, as is necessary for friends who must share an activity. Julie says that they will share their destinies, even if fortune is cruel enough to separate them.

Julie's confidence in their shared destiny provides her with the strength to claim authority over St. Preux. She can now depend on his obedience rather than his virtue. The establishment of authority and obedience is an important development between them. Authority can be established because there is a common good or shared destiny that assures the ruled that he will not be subjected to a tyranny, that Julie will not be capricious. She claims to rule for the happiness of both, and gives reasons for why her rule is more apt to secure their happiness. Now that their hearts are united, it is a matter of prudence to ensure that they are able to live together. And since she is more prudent than the passionate St. Preux, it follows that she should rule. But, we cannot help noticing that she thinks his happiness is more easily separated from hers than vice versa. The union of body and soul, that he longs for, threatens her honor. The common good has a questionable character.

St. Preux readily consents to be ruled by Julie. He is not hesitant because he believes that a benevolent heart such as Julie's could rule only for his good. Her benevolent authority promises to reward him for his obedience. Her understanding of their relation reflects the relation of God to man in paradise. He does not fear her rule, but trusts like a child. And if his obedience is in any way painful, it is eased by the promise of reward.

The idea of authority and obedience in matters of love implies inequality and hierarchy. Rousseau denies that equality is required for respect, and he denies that authority is necessarily tyrannical. He thinks that the relation between male and female is not that of master and slave, but he rejects equality as the mediating principle between them. The respect, accompanying sexual relatedness, cannot be the respect for an equal. Equality and respect for human beings as human beings might keep people from murdering one another for their religious beliefs, which is how it got its footing, but it is absurd and perverse as a part of sexual relatedness. It is perverse because sexuality relates one to a particular person. Respect for the abstract person is nothing but a protest and prayer against the dishonor, indifference, and brutality of sex without love.

There is no possibility of love without modesty, just as there is no possibility of modesty without the hope of love. Rousseau knows that modesty is often criticized for betraying its true motives, either self-protection, sexual desire, or concern for reputation. But, he denies that it can be reduced to any of the three. Julie is willing to sacrifice all three, at one time or another, for the sake of love. Female modesty contains within it an awareness of the eternal order. It provides an idea, image, and sentiment of a common good to which men and women belong. That is why love can be divinized as something beyond the lovers.

Julie's first use of her authority takes place because innocence is lost and virtue is weak. Julie wanted to sweeten St. Preux's condition of restraint by rewarding him; she gives him a kiss. This one kiss creates a crisis with which they will struggle for the rest of their lives. Julie did not know that kisses between lovers are never innocent, and that, if one is to remain virtuous, the senses must be denied entirely. Her inexperience, coupled with her pity and gratitude, lead her down the path from which there is no turning back. Just as the fall of man from God's grace does not lead back to Eden, but to law and virtue, so, too, Julie's fall will lead to morality and romantic longing for a lost past.

The kiss has disturbed both St. Preux and Julie. She fainted upon contact, and his senses disturb his fragile equanimity. Julie uses her authority in an attempt to preserve them from themselves. She sends St. Preux on a journey through the Swiss Alps, where he had always wanted to travel. The plan is a success to the extent that St. Preux's passion is purified. The grandeur of the Alps, the variety of landscapes and vegetation, and the purity of the air raise him above sensuality. But she requests that he return because his absence, coupled with her father's command that she marry Wolmar, oppresses her hope almost to the point of death. His proximity to her rekindles his hope of being with her and, therefore, the pain of frustrated happiness and anger at fate. They are both miserable and seek relief from their pains.

Julie gives up her virtue in order to avoid harming her lover and disobeying her father. The consummation of their love is not the joyous occasion anticipated by St. Preux. He is degraded by her tears. He thinks that she is crying over the loss of her virtue, and there is some truth to his speculation. She would like to cry forever, to never be consoled for the loss of something so dear to her and on which she thought her esteem depended. She would be a coquette not to have cried, and a stone not to be consoled. St. Preux attempts to persuade her that she does no dishonor to herself, provided that she only does it with him. The exclusivity of love and the fidelity of friendship replace chastity. She tells him that the loss of her virginity is not the reason for her tears, but rather the degradation of their love. She thinks that they are no different from beasts and common lovers whose pleasures are sensual frenzies lacking in tenderness and blessedness.

Julie's tears soon dry and she looks forward to both the pleasures of love and the hope of legitimating them. She also finds, despite her protests, that she is jealous. She does not try to root jealousy out of her soul because it is a selfish passion. She knows that jealousy and love are inseparable. Jealousy need not consist of self-righteous accusations and vindictive punishments, as it is portrayed in plays like Euripides' *Medea* and Shakespeare's *Othello*. Jealousy is first experienced as the pain of doubt, which comes from the possibility that the one whom one loves loves someone else. Julie's jealousy would torment herself alone, thereby, turning her greatest joy into her greatest torment. She would suffer from suspicions that she would keep to herself, and that would poison her love, even though they are unsupported. In order to guard against this frightful passion, or at least against suffering from it without reason, she makes St. Preux promise that, if his heart should fall to another, then he ought to tell her immediately. His promise relieves her of her fears, for she knows that while he could be a faithless lover (since love depends on the faithless heart), he could never be a false friend. St. Preux is also jealous, despite his protests to the contrary, and he asks for a similar oath from Julie. She promises to marry no one without his consent, but she will not marry him without her father's consent. The belief in their shared destinies requires oaths now that they are no longer innocents.

The oaths between Julie and St. Preux are a prelude to their second and final rendezvous. The first experience was predominately a relief from desperation, but it taught them something about what they wanted. Rousseau has Julie's parents leave for a week so that we might see what effect pleasure has had on the two lovers. They are confronted by a choice between the pleasures of love and performing a charitable deed. Fanchon, a poor girl and Julie's ward, has fallen into destitution. Her father has injured himself and is unable to earn money. She is faced with the shameful prospect of taking public assistance, becoming a mistress, or of accepting money from a suitor (Claude Anet), who has sold himself as a mercenary in order to support her. Julie is filled with pity for Fanchon, admiration for Claude, and reproach for herself. She commands St. Preux to purchase the freedom of Claude so that he can marry Fanchon. This deed can be considered moral because they actually sacrifice something to perform it.

St. Preux obeys Julie's command because she is beneficent, and because he must have her respect. She loves him even more for putting a good deed and her respect above his own pleasures. And, once again, he is to be rewarded for his virtue. They plan another rendezvous at a festivity in honor of Fanchon's marriage, but Julie is detained by her mother. Julie's frustration transforms her into a daring lover. She calls her mother cruel, and plans a rendezvous in her father's house, knowing that, if they are discovered, it will be death for both of them. Her frustrated longing raises her spirit and heightens the pitch of her desire. She will snatch happiness at least once before she dies. Here, she resembles St. Preux, the Platonic lover, who seeks to overcome his low fortune and partake of true being through love. This is an anticipated moment for both.

Julie's modesty does not permit her to write about their love, but St. Preux's thoughts and feelings are freely given. St. Preux says what is incomprehensible to the enlightened Parisians: the ecstasies, for which he would give a thousand lives, are less dear to him than the languishing tenderness following them. The greatest pleasures of love are not the most intensive ones. The dearest moment takes place after the satisfaction of desire. St. Preux declares that he could now die knowing that he has tasted happiness and that nothing more awaits him. His satisfaction and freedom is characterized by him as an experience of being; he believes that his soul has taken hold of an eternal possession. The universal and particular come together for him in the possession of Julie. Their mutual possession provides him with an experience of being that is independent, or, at least, is experienced as such, of their particularity. His experience gives him a standard of beauty and truth that he will take with him to his grave.

His experience is meant as an alternative to science and hedonism. He challenges materialists to look inside his heart and tell him that he does not feel what he feels. His experience is a revelation with Julie as his prophet, and love as his god. The truth is not an abstraction for him, nor is his direct experience of it animal or philistine. His happiness will be lost for conventional as well as natural reasons, but he will never doubt the character of the absolute moment.

Just as the kiss was followed by a crisis and separation, so, too, St. Preux's moment of happiness is but a flash of lightning that is followed by misery. It is now that Bomston insults Julie and begins a series of events that will ultimately lead to Julie's renunciation of love as an illusion that mistakes passion for virtue. The movement from the revelation to Julie's disavowal separates the truth from the possibility of earthly happiness for St. Preux. This separation requires either the rethinking of what was thought to be the fundamental experience, the break with the attachment to Julie or the reunion of the two through a promise in the afterlife. Bomston's insult helps immediately in laying bare the problem. What seemed like a perfect unity between the possession of love and the possession of Julie, now appears like a disunity. St. Preux avenges her honor and the truth as one would avenge an insult against one's god. But, as anyone who is familiar with philosophy knows, defending the honor of one's god conflicts with ideas about God. God is supposed to be self-sufficient; he does not need human beings to avenge Him, or even to worship Him. Defending His honor is really defending one's own love for Him. But, vengeance would not be necessary if one possessed the beloved eternally in its perfection. The disunity between divinized love and the particular beloved is the conflict of the lover. Rousseau's romanticism is one way of solving the problem. It promises a return to the state of blessed love in return for the sacrifices made to its god. Romanticism is a sensualized version of man's fall and redemption.

The crisis allows St. Preux to make another sacrifice; he agrees to be exiled rather than to run the risk of ruining Julie's reputation. But, the emphasis on reputation is Claire's rather than Julie's. Julie is more concerned with disobeying a clearly stated command of her father not to see St. Preux. The protection of reputation is one of the offices of friendship. The concern with reputation is more akin to the friend's concern with virtue and well-being than to the self-forgetting madness of the lover. Nonetheless, St. Preux is prevailed upon to sacrifice his happiness in order to preserve his worthiness. How could he be worthy if he were to put his happiness before Julie's? Like earlier sacrifices, however, it is accompanied by accusations of ingratitude against Julie. He is both indignant and cold when reflecting upon the causes of their separation. His heart hardens into indifference upon the prospect of an eternal separation. But, his anger eventually finds expression. He accuses Julie of giving scant consideration to his happiness and misery while he makes sacrifices for her.

Once again, Julie restores his hope and assuages his anger. But, this is the beginning of the end; she will finally break with him. The genesis of this break was discussed in chapter 2. The reasons for the break reveal the fundamental conflict in Julie's life (a conflict different from St. Preux's), and prepares the transition from love to family.

While Julie puts forth the first principles of the family, St. Preux attempts to cure himself of despair, or die. He heads for the sea. The vastness of the ocean and its isolation provide the appropriate stage for his condition. He is confronted with the forces of an angry world where, if he should drown, he would be forever lost. Yet, although St. Preux's despair is dear to him, for it confirms the depth of his love, he survives it. The ocean does not engulf him; he does not commit suicide; nor is he drained of his will to live. St. Preux's voyage is equivalent to Julie's conversion in so far as he learns to survive an unhappy love. He differs from Julie in that he must learn to live with an unhappy love, whereas she falls out of love. His courage is restored to him in the classic manner: he is forced to witness the depths to which human beings can sink and the hardship that can befall them. The suffering and brutality of master-slave relations, the greed and terror of piracy and imperial wars, as well as the horror on a man's face as he is swallowed by the sea are all sights he has digested. The worst sights he saw in Paris were poverty and libertinism.

The degradation, injustices, and horrors to which St. Preux is witness do not turn him into a misanthrope or a revolutionary. Upon his return he declares that he has never seen anything as extraordinary as the souls of Julie and Claire, and that neither time, nor distance, can erase the impressions they have left on him. They preserve his heart from anger and melancholy just as the pity and shame he feels for mankind preserves him from his despair. His travels extend the range of his sympathies, thereby taking him out of himself without destroying his dearest attachments; he returns, still in love, but with a manly awareness of the suffering and brutality that is coeval with man. The contrast between the state of war and the friendship between Julie and Claire cannot help but relieve him, in part, of his desire to possess Julie because she is a marvel in a world where virtue rarely shines through the clouds of corruption and savagery.

St. Preux's previous journeys also suited the state of his heart and are also introductions to the society of Clarens. He first arrives in Vevey as an innocent who has never felt love. His first expression of it is a confession. He travels to the Upper Valais at a time when he has kissed his beloved, but has not possessed her. He can be charmed by innocence, but is inspired by love. And he travels to Paris after he has possessed Julie. He knows love and is, therefore, in a position to judge the pleasures of the big city.

St. Preux's travels are fitted not only to his ability for sympathetic and critical evaluation of social arrangements, but are meant to be examples of different parts of the whole. Vevey is dominated by God, Valais is dominated by nature, and Paris is dominated by reason. Clarens is meant to be a beautiful harmony between nature, reason, and piety. Birth and death in Clarens are accompanied by inner feelings of attachment that have been informed by Greek philosophy and Christianity. Authority there does not stifle reason and nature; reason has not dissolved human attachments and duty; and nature has not been left untutored, without reflection on the whole or appreciation of beauty. Clarens is meant to be an example of the good society where there is nothing lacking to human happiness.

Clarens first comes to sight as a society that is both ordered and free. Both Shklar and Starobinski are impressed by its natural freedom and equality, and its paternalism. Shklar concentrates her discussion on Wolmar and his relation to the peasants, while Starobinski concentrates his discussion on the grape harvest.[2] And while Shklar compares Wolmar to the legislator in the *Social Contract*, and finds Wolmar's rule closer to nature, Starobinski compares the grape harvest to the state of nature and finds Clarens more conventional. The comparisons of Clarens with the state of nature and political society are helpful for situating it somewhere between nature and society, but they are too far removed from it to give the kind of contrast required for definition. Clarens needs to be contrasted with the other societies in the novel, and it needs to be examined as part of the dramatic conflict between love and family.

Clarens contains the paternalism and class distinctions of Vevey, the natural goodness of the Upper Valais, the intelligence and enjoyment of beauty found in Paris, and, like Geneva, there is a common good, even though the sexes have different tasks. Clarens is both free and cultured.

The parts of Clarens are differentiated by class and sex. It is not necessary to go into the details of how Wolmar rules the peasants, but it is important to understand that they do not obey authority backed by force. They have inner feelings, which confirm to them that they belong to Clarens as a whole, and their place in it. Clarens differs from Sparta because the integration of the parts into an order does not require, as a matter of course, the sacrifice of one's life. It differs from a cosmopolitan city like Paris because there is an order. The peasants and the children require very little in the way of reflection and reasoning about their experience and the world to accept their place. The same cannot be said of Julie, St. Preux, and Wolmar. The latter give the society its tone and its reason for being.

Rousseau says that it is the nature of the peasant to do what his father before him did.[3] It is not the nature of the peasant to question the order of things because he does not, like St. Preux, have an education and elevated sentiments that bring him into conflict with them and cause him to think about the best order of things. The peasants are more likely to be brought into conflict with authority through stealing and debauchery rather than through a claim to justice. They are corrupted through examples of vice (often those of their master), which make them useless and vicious. The nobler types have more need of having their opinions integrated into Clarens than do the peasants. Their education is more negative than positive. Foremost to their education is keeping them from examples of vice and the opportunity of falling into it.

Although the peasants are not equal, they are far from being treated like animals or slaves. They are elevated by inequality because they can share, if only in a limited sense, in the beauty and honor of the peaks. Of course, the inequality alone does not necessitate the binding of the bottom to the top. The social order must connect the top with the bottom while keeping them separate. The peasants must be rewarded for their work, and they must not be held in contempt. Wolmar is not afraid to work in the fields, attend their festivals, and even, despite his atheism, go to church with them. The work, pleasures, and distinctions of their rank are never treated with disdain. The benefits they enjoy would not be sufficient to maintain a familial society if they were not accompanied by enough shared humanity and personal attachment to enable the peasants to share in the good fortune and honor of the Wolmars.

St. Preux implicitly suggests that the order at Clarens is unjust. He does not make an argument about the justice of equality, nor does his complaint include an understanding of the order and ends of government. In a discussion about the education of Julie's children, St. Preux objects that they are not educated with a view to their talents. He suggests that the education of the peasants is unjust because they are educated with an eye toward their class rather than their abilities. Julie does not make an attempt to justify aristocracy as such, but simply says that education ought not to have as its goal the cultivation of talents. Her argument has many sound reflections on the formation of reason and character, but is primarily an indictment of cosmopolitanism. The core of the argument is that those talents have meaning only if they culminate in the true genius who is capable of teaching mankind his duties. But this man will cultivate himself, despite a lack of encouragement, as the example of Rousseau's own life makes clear. Furthermore, the peasants are more likely to be corrupted by an education that does not prepare them for the life they are most likely to live and which is the most decent alternative for them. Talents are only of use in the city, and that is where many go to find pleasure and fortune, only to find their ruin. The aristocrats could help to keep them in the country by cultivating more of their land.

Julie's criticism of education, directed toward talent, helps to reveal the character of Clarens. She does not make an argument for the superiority of aristocracy to equality and freedom, but she implicitly defends the order she lives in by looking at the immediate alternatives. Clarens is a rural aristocracy that no longer requires force to establish and defend itself, nor the justifications which accompany its use. Wolmar's reform, and the common good of Clarens, depend upon habits of belief.

Clarens is like the Upper Valais in that it is not commercial. It is a subsistence farm that does not corrupt its members through the opportunity to make money and to pursue material goods. It differs from the Upper Valais because it contains class differences. The Upper Valais is a rustic republic, while Clarens is a rustic aristocracy. Yet, despite its hierarchy, it is like Geneva in so far as it is a little polis that is greater than the sum of its parts.

The Upper Valais does not have households in the strict sense of the term. The women are servants and the men are providers. They are not two parts contributing to a greater whole. At Clarens, as at Geneva, the different tasks of the sexes contribute to a unity that is greater than the sum of its parts. Yet, Rousseau does not follow Aristotle, who reformed the patriarchy of the household by making it an image of the political.[4] Aristotle also gives to the household a common good, but he finds the equitableness of the relations between male and female less in complementary virtues and felt sentiment than in the justice of giving each what he or she deserves. Clarens is close enough to nature to need no law about the just distribution of places, but it is removed enough to have a common good.

The major distinction other than class, within the society of Clarens, is that of gender, and it is this distinction that gives the household its unity. Men and women are understood in Clarens almost as different species with their own virtues and pleasures. They are very proud and jealous of their differences and form different societies where the other is unsuited and unwelcome. The women are not allowed to compete with the men at their games, and the men are not allowed to join the women for cake and conversation in the nursery. Clarens is a sexist society: the women work in the house and look after the children and the men work the land. The division of labor has everything to do with the differences between their bodies. The men are stronger and, therefore, more suited to hard labor. The women give birth and have a more immediate attachment to babies and children, and are therefore, more suited to caring for them and educating them. The differences in body and labor are so determinative that they even find expression in their taste for food and drink. Where the men do not have a taste for the bitter, and the women do not have a taste for the sweet, Rousseau suggests that the social order is corrupt.

The differentiation of the sexes in the household, as practiced in Clarens, differs from the differentiation required for love because the household separates the sexes rather than uniting them. Husband and wife do not live for one another; they live for their children and the moral order which supports that attachment. The separation of the sexes in the household discourages the permissiveness that brings disorder into households and undermines the sacredness of the child. The modesty of Julie, the lover, and that of Julie, the wife and mother, are two different virtues. The latter is more closely connected with social virtue and must, therefore, be more concerned with appearances.

The differentiation of the sexes at Clarens has, no doubt, a basis in economics. The provision of food and shelter is the task of the men, while the women prepare it and maintain it, respectively. What makes Clarens more than just a group of drudges helping one another to survive is the influence of the Wolmars, especially Julie. Her modesty and tenderness give the men and the women an idea of virtue and happiness. The men, like St. Preux, are more afraid of her displeasure than of Wolmar's severity, and it breaks Julie's heart to have to deny them her affection on account of their errors. The women pride themselves on being different from the men; it flatters them greatly that the master of the house is not permitted entrance into the nursery. They share in the respect due to Julie. Despite Julie's need to appear beyond suspicion, she is still able to inspire tender affection. She is seen walking with Wolmar and she enjoys dancing at the festivities. Julie could not exert a similar influence in Geneva because, there, the separation of the sexes is not mitigated by tenderness. The influence of politics and commerce makes it impossible for a female to be the centre of their society. While it is true that the household is Wolmar's, it is, nonetheless, true that Clarens is not ruled by a father, made in the image of a jealous god, who considers his wife, children, and servants as his property. Reason rules in Clarens to the extent that the common good and happiness are the aim of the association.

Clarens must be understood as more than an example of a social order made up of different classes and genders. It is, above all, part of a personal story. Wolmar, Julie, and St. Preux are the principal characters of the household. The *ménage à trois* is a common theme in Rousseau's works. In *The Confessions*, there are several examples from Rousseau's own life, and in *La Nouvelle Héloïse* there are other less pronounced examples. Rousseau believes that this situation is important to an understanding of the human situation. We must turn to Wolmar for an understanding of the man responsible for the situation.

Wolmar is clearly Rousseau's variation on Plato's philosopher-king and the biblical God. He is an atheist who rules for the common good, but he is also a father who seems omniscient and omnipresent and whose existence requires children.[5] Wolmar cannot be understood without contrasting his passionate attachments with Plato's philosopher-king, and his lack of righteous authority with that of the biblical God.

Wolmar is the most philosophic of the men. He is the classic atheist, an Epicurean materialist. He loves order and observation and would become a living eye if he could. He was born a prince, but left the court at an early age to study human beings. He even became a serf in order to understand them. He is by temperament, and perhaps to some extent from station, free from passionate attachment. The destruction of his kingdom is not even a cause for his concern. He returns to salvage what he can and then leaves without any sense of loss. He is almost above passion; he is an image of the divine, which is free from the body, and which partakes of constancy and eternity through its apprehension of necessity. He does not belong to anyone, nor to any place. His temperament and thought help to explain why he can bring his wife's ex-lover into his household. But the question remains: "Why would a philosopher become a husband and father?"

Upon approaching the age of fifty, Wolmar feels the need for a tender attachment. This is the spark, which leads to his life with Julie. The aging Wolmar begins to feel the cold hand of death (not to mention the prospect of old age without assistance), and longs for an attachment that will keep him from the abyss. His atheism is at odds with his heart. He is not aware of the contradiction in his life and will come to know it only when circumstances reveal it to him. Wolmar sheds tears for the first time in his life when he and Julie share in the mutual, though silent, recognition that she has no hope to recover from her illness. His tears are prayers and a harbinger of his conversion. They are a relief and a consolation for a personal pain that cannot be looked at with a theoretical eye. Wolmar cannot believe that man is alone, that the truth about his existence does not have a place for a god and an afterlife. Wolmar is, like Rousseau's Emile, the closest approximation to a philosopher without being one.

Wolmar's attempt to continue himself through his children, as well as his belief in a god who cares for the fate of human beings sets him apart from Plato's philosopher-king, who must be forced to concern himself with the affairs of individuals. His attachments are more characteristic of the biblical God, who is a jealous God, because he loves and wants to be loved. But, Wolmar's attachment to his wife and children is not accompanied by a righteous law. He does not create a moral order in support of his right to obedient love, although he is subtly jealous. He believes that Julie's doubts about her own virtue insult him. Certainly, Julie knows that her death confession, which essentially calls her life with Wolmar a lie, will be painful to him. Wolmar's jealousy never transforms itself into righteous authority, in part, because of his tranquil character, his materialistic philosophy, and his analytic and reflective disposition. But, these are not sufficient reasons because his passionate attachment is more determinative for him than his reason. The fact that Wolmar married Julie against her will, and with full knowledge that she loved St. Preux, puts him in the position of having to justify himself to her. He says that, in his heart, he knew that he was the only man who could make her happy. He must be more interested in her happiness than his rights if he is to justify the marriage; after all, he does not believe in the sacredness of the wedding vows nor in the sacredness of the child. The divine law against adultery is, in his eyes, the consequence of maternal love and honor, rather than paternal jealousy and strength.

Part of Wolmar's justification of his marriage is that passionate love does not bring happiness, for he could never be an object of passionate love. He is a man of considerable probity, though less than St. Preux, and needs to believe that the happiness of his wife is not a mere appearance. His invitation of St. Preux into the household is part of his proof. His entire exercise is a failure, that reveals his selfishness and the mistaking of appearance for reality. As Julie claimed to see the error of her ways when renouncing St. Preux, Wolmar learns his when Julie renounces him. Julie needs a god within her. She has the opinion that the tranquillity of marriage ought to make her happy, but she feels the need for an enthusiastic state. The devotion she once gave to love, she gives to God when married. Her death letter, confessing her love for St. Preux, sheds light on the failure of Wolmar's plan.

Wolmar's jealousy does not turn into a righteous law primarily because he believes that he has the ability to make himself loved. He thinks that he can cure people of faithlessness and temptation through his friendship, wisdom, and the manipulation of their imagination. His love of sincerity is, if not fully known to him, a means by which he attaches others to him and keeps them honest. He actually has a method for sincerity. When one is speaking to him, one ought to pretend that he is not there, and when he is not there, one ought to pretend that he is there. This is an approximation of the general will and the inspiration for Kant's understanding of morality. Wolmar's instruction in sincerity has the advantage of always making himself present, like the biblical God, for one cannot imagine that the person before oneself is not there. Wolmar resembles the omnipresent God who inspires loyalty because of his benevolence and because one cannot escape from being reminded of it.

Wolmar is not only omnipresent, but omniscient as well. He attempts to inspire obedience through the awe of a revelation. He takes Julie and St. Preux to the very spot where they had their first fatal kiss. By taking them to that spot, he, no doubt, makes them feel guilt before him, like Adam and Eve after they had eaten from the tree of knowledge. But, their guilt is not disobedience, and it is not to be punished, though Wolmar will certainly take advantage of it. Wolmar chooses this spot to give a revelation. He reveals to them that he has read their letters. He, thus, lays them naked before him. He does not, however, use their nakedness to shame them; he attempts to inspire them, for he also reveals to them his divine plan to cure St. Preux of his love and to have him educate his children. They are worthy of his plan because they gave up a moment of pleasure in order to assist Fanchon and Claude; they did not put their pleasures above humanity. They are, therefore, worthy of his efforts, which will require them to live as brother and sister. Wolmar also reveals to them the story of his life. Julie did not know that he (Wolmar) was a prince, nor did she know, although she suspected, that he never felt tenderness until seeing her, and that the desire to possess her was the first passion he ever felt. His revelation is meant to inspire awe, faith, and love. It is, of course, a failure, as the conclusion of the novel demonstrates. It is a failure, not only because Julie calls their life a lie, but also because she dies before he does. Wolmar's plan did not seek divine assistance; he thought that he could conquer fortune, but fortune conquers him. Julie's death confutes him and converts him.

Although Julie and St. Preux do not betray Wolmar's trust, they nonetheless, lose their faith. The heart has its own laws; supreme love cannot be compelled, even through gratitude. In keeping with her gratitude, Julie believes that a just God would not punish a just man like Wolmar, but it is with St. Preux that she hopes to be reunited for eternity. The Bible must bend to her righteousness and love rather than vice versa. Julie's confession of love for St. Preux should not come as a surprise. There are many indications that show Wolmar's plan was causing torment and was likely to fail. Before Julie's death, she was experiencing the torment of conflicting passions that temporarily destroyed her reason earlier in her life. The fear of being alone with St. Preux, the tears she sheds upon witnessing the monument of St. Preux's love, and the zealous attempt to marry him to Claire, are all clear indications of the state of her soul. Her death is a relief from the torment of her life. She dies with a final reconciliation between her love of St. Preux and morality. Heaven is a refuge for lovers who have sacrificed their happiness in order to be worthy of it. Hell does not exist, and she is, therefore, free from the fear of Wolmar's eternal damnation and the guilt of forsaking a condemned husband. Her religion makes sense of her life by promising her a happiness she had to disavow in life.

St. Preux is cured of his love no more than Julie. Certainly, Julie's confession will awaken his suppressed hopes. Wolmar thought that the most effective way to cure St. Preux of his love was to present him with an image of Julie as Madame Wolmar, the wife of his friend and the mother of his friend's children. It is effective within limits. St. Preux has reveries about his past happiness, and he wears the miniature portrait of Julie next to his heart. Wolmar takes this to mean that he has separated the past from the present. But, the revery of the past would lose its attraction if the past was thought to be gone; it is necessarily accompanied by illusions and hopes of reunion and rejuvenation.

St. Preux is so far from being cured that he attempts to reawaken the glory of love in Julie. Wolmar leaves Julie and St. Preux to themselves for one week. In order not to be alone with St. Preux, Julie arranges a boat ride. A storm forces them onto the shores of Meillerie near the cliffs and cave where St. Preux lived as a desperate lover and threatened suicide. The cave is a shrine containing monuments to his love. The instruments by which he made his engravings have been left untouched. Upon witnessing the place, St. Preux becomes enthusiastic; he is full of passionate memories and hope. Julie does not share his celebration. She returns with him to the boat, and then they leave for home. On the boat, Julie sheds tears for her lost love. These tears anger St. Preux because he feels that fate is denying him a happiness he deserves. He must distance himself from Julie on the boat because he has a powerful urge to drown her with himself. He is tempted to destroy both of them to spite fate, but he will eventually quench his anger with tears.

St. Preux's dreams about Julie's death also betray him. These dreams take place on the way to Italy where Bomston intends to test his fitness to be part of Wolmar's household to see if he will place the good of a friend above his own passion. St. Preux dreams that Julie's face is covered by a veil that cannot be lifted from her face. His dream is an intimation of her death. She is separated from him, and despite all his efforts, there is no possibility of establishing the first condition of togetherness—an awareness of one another. His dream causes him to think that something terrible has happened to Julie; he is debilitated by his fear. Bomston takes the stoic role once again by attempting to cure him of his fear. As a teacher, he is the obverse of Wolmar who tries to cure St. Preux of his love. Bomston takes St. Preux back to Clarens without him knowing it. St. Preux's fear for Julie is moderated by the fear of being laughed at, but it is not enough to calm him. He overcomes his fear of ridicule and his fear of the dream through the good luck of overhearing Julie speaking to Claire. Once he knows that Julie is alive, he leaves again for Italy without having announced his presence. Bomston's cure is similar to Wolmar's in its attempt to cure a passion through the presentation of a new image. Ironically, St. Preux believes that the dream and its cure have cured him not only of his fear, but also of his love. The horror of her death makes her life dearer to him than his love. A lover would not have this sentiment. A lover, true to the epigram placed at the front of the book, would think that his heart alone knows her. Wolmar's images do not seem to be as effective as the image of death. But, even the image of death will not cure St. Preux of his love because his love is needed to cure him of the horror of death. Bomston's cure is a temporary one, just as is marriage and family for Julie. We never hear from St. Preux after Julie's death. He is ill, and his pain is beyond the relief of words. We are left to surmise that his salvation is the same as Julie's—the hope for reunion in the afterlife.

St. Preux pays a heavy price for avoiding the ridicule of Julie and Claire upon his return to Clarens; he missed his last chance of ever seeing Julie again. The pain of his despair avenges his insult to love, as his shame avenged his earlier crime at the brothel. Lovers are not permitted to free themselves from the wounded pride of being laughed at. They are supposed to find strength of character in the attachment to the beloved; they have no independent pride. Julie's death conquers St. Preux's pride and independence. Love is his only relief from her death.

The conclusion of *La Nouvelle Héloïse* has the effect of arousing subdued indignation in addition to pity and hope. It does not seem just that these two lovers should have been denied on earth what they hope for in heaven. But, under Rousseau's tutelage, our indignation is not likely to be as confident and fierce as was Bomston's. Rousseau has taken us through the complexity of private attachments, and if he has not made us too wise to be indignant, he has, at least, taught moderation by making us aware of the conflict between love and morality. This conflict should also cure us of the inclination to think of love and family as a natural union simply because the latter is a natural consequence of the former. Mothers and fathers do not sigh over one another.

Rousseau thought that the completion promised by love and by family to be mutually exclusive. No one took to heart Rousseau's dichotomy more than Tolstoy. *Anna Karenina* is, following *La Nouvelle Héloïse*, almost to a period, a book about love and a book about family. The difference is that Tolstoy sides with family against love. The simple desire to do good, that is characteristic of the Russian peasant and a tender mother, is the climactic revelation that takes the place of Julie's avowal and expectation of love. Tolstoy attempts to give the simple soul the flavor of love by presenting its goodness as a joyous answer to despairing doubts. Would its simplicity alone suffice to satisfy the longing for eternity?

While Tolstoy lends enthusiasm to the familial, he drains love of its divine character. Unlike Rousseau, he does not sacrifice happiness to love in order to preserve it. He portrays love through an adulterous affair, and he subjects the lovers to the inevitable problems of illegitimate birth, familiarity, and bodily decay. Rousseau is truer to the sentiment of love because he sacrifices happiness in order to preserve its sweet hope. Anna's suicide does not accompany the hope for happiness. She kills herself in order to satisfy her jealousy; her suicide reveals her passionate attachment, but that attachment is poisoned by self-pity and vindictiveness. Her death elevates her to tragic proportions, but it does not express the highest hopes of love. In *La Nouvelle Héloïse*, love outlives its sensual satisfactions through its longing for the past. The return to Eden is not a return to innocent bliss under the watchful eye of a loving father, but a return to wholeness through union with one's beloved.

NOTES

1. *La Nouvelle Héloïse*, I, xlvi, p. 128.
2. Judith Shkar, *Men and Citizens: A Study of Rousseau's Social Theory* (Cambridge, 1969), pp. 130–51. Jean Starobinski, *Jean Jacques Rousseau: Transparency and Ob-straction*, trans. Goldhammer (Chicago, 1988), pp. 88–111.
3. *Emile*, p. 118.
4. Aristotle, *Politics*, trans. Lord, (Chicago, 1984), 1253b1.
5. See Joel Schwartz, *The Sexual Politics of Jean-Jacques Rous-seau* (Chicago, 1985), p. 173, n. 11.

Conclusion

Love and family have two different meanings that correspond to the two different characters of intercourse and procreation, respectively, though neither can be comprehended by their bodily origins alone. Love is more directed toward pleasure than preservation, while the opposite is true of family. Love promises supreme happiness, whereas family provides order and tranquility. Neither, however, can be exclusively characterized by longing and contentment, respectively, because the longings of love culminate in an experience of possession and the tranquility of family is disturbed by death. St. Preux believes that he has tasted true happiness, and Wolmar comes to believe in God and the afterlife.

Love and family are not only different, but are in irreconcilable conflict with one another. This conflict is most evident in Julie's renunciations and returns. At one time, she declares that love is an illusion and gives it up for family, and, at another time, she declares family an illusion and renounces it for love. These contradictions are not caused by indecisiveness or capriciousness, but are reflections of the incoherence that the dual aspects of sexuality pose for civil man. Julie contains within her this conflict more than either St. Preux or Wolmar because the duality of intercourse and procreation are by nature more inherent to the female than the male. Even as a young girl in love she lives in relation to the children to whom she has yet to have given birth.

Although Julie's connection to her children places a limit on what she is willing to sacrifice to love, that connection does not, by itself, provide a motive and justification for the family. The sacredness of marriage and the child, and the corresponding laws against adultery and parricide, are made sensible to Julie through the terror of annihilation, or, at least, the closest thing to it that she can imagine.

The horror she feels at the image of an unmourned death, specifically, that of her father, teaches her the limits of love and provides the background for her return to God. Through death and birth, Julie partakes of the terror and awe inspired by God's acts of destruction and creation. The horror of death also provides Wolmar with a motive, though not a reason, to form a family. His marriage to Julie gives him a tender attachment that keeps him from despair, and his children give him an image of continuity that places a barrier between himself and nothing. Family, unlike love, is not immediately connected to the sensual organs. The maternal instinct, which is the most immediate connection between par-

ent and child, is never felt by the father, nor by the mother during con-
ception. The fear of death, understood as being detached from others and
oneself, is the determinative passion for the family, as the desire for intercourse is the determinative passion for love. The fear of death not only
informs the maternal instinct, which is necessary for the survival of the
species, but it also informs the desire for self-preservation. Children are
an extension of oneself into the future. The order and tranquility of family is to no small extent a reaction to the abyss.

Lovers do not require children. In fact, children make love impossible.
Lovers belong to one another; they do not belong to part of a larger
society. Consequently, lovers do not live by laws. They require divine
witness to their oaths, but not divine punishment. Law requires force and
generality, whereas love requires freedom and the belief in the unique-
ness of the lovers. Property plays no essential part in the lives of lovers. It
is merely something that is to be shared between them or given away
altogether. The family is more closely connected to property and ideas of
justice because it is less concerned with pleasure and supreme happiness
than with preservation and continuity. If the child is to be sacred, and it
must be if it is to contain an image of oneself that reassures oneself of
one's own immortality, then birth must be a determinative act that gives
reason to intercourse as well as to ideas of belonging and property. The
family, unlike love, requires an order that defends and defines what is
one's own to the exclusion of others. Love is never a matter for justice,
because it is never a matter for force. Lovers cannot compel one another
to love, and they cannot justify their love by appealing to the authority of
the law.

Love and family are not only in conflict with one another, but also
with nature and reason. They partake of nature in so far as they are
founded on intercourse and procreation, and they partake of reason in so
far as they are associations formed around experiences accessible to human beings as human beings, rather than through a particular scriptural
authority. Their affinity with nature and reason is evident by their differences with Christian piety, aristocratic honor, and patriarchal authority.
Love and family are more sensual and bodily in their attachments than
are those of Christianity; they are not solely dependant upon the opinions
of others as are those of aristocratic honor; and, they are more sentimental and humane than are the ones founded on patriarchal authority. Love
and family share with reason and nature, respectively, a degree of generality and independence from opinion.

But, in light of reason and nature, love and family are hypocritical and
deluded. They seem hypocritical because their members claim to be subordinated to the union, when, in fact, traces of natural selfishness are
evident. And, they seem unreasonable because the happiness they promise is founded on illusions. St. Preux's sacrifices are always accompanied
by claims to desert, as well as the hope for recognition and reward, if not

in this life, certainly in the afterlife. When he loses hope he becomes desperate, as when he wanted to drown Julie with himself, and as when he wanted to commit suicide. Furthermore, when he thinks that his sacrifices are not being recognized, he becomes indignant at his unjust treatment, as when Julie did not answer his letters, and as when he banished himself from Vevey. His hopes and claims to desert throw a question mark over the nobility of his sacrifices. In fact, some of his actions, themselves, are of a questionable character. He is so sure that his happiness coincides with Julie's and that love is the meaning of life, that he imprudently and selfishly tries to reawaken love in Julie after she has married Wolmar. When they are storm tossed on to Meillerie, he shows her relics and inscriptions of his love, even though she is the wife of his friend and the mother of his friend's children.

The self-serving aspect of St. Preux's sacrifices are not only hypocritical, but deluded, when seen from the perspective of reason's universality and atheism. The beauty he perceives in Julie has its source in himself. Modesty is the thread out of which all her other virtues are woven. But, modesty is derivative from love. Modesty depends on the desire for a permanent and exclusive attachment. This desire makes the virtue of the beloved dependant on the possibility of satisfying the desire of the lover, as is evident from St. Preux's complaints and hopes. His perception of beauty is, therefore, an illusion because it has its source in his desires, rather than the object of his love. Furthermore, St. Preux's belief in God and the afterlife are, likewise, beautifications of his desire, as they preserve the beauty of his beloved by preserving her from decay, and as they preserve the hope to be united with her forever.

Wolmar's beneficence, like St. Preux's sacrifices, are also self-regarding and founded on illusions, but, while St. Preux's sublimated selfishness is that of a devotee, Wolmar's is that of a god. Wolmar gives in order to receive. He marries Julie with full knowledge of her love for St. Preux because he needs a tender attachment to soften the cold hand of death. He also wants children for the same reason; they give him an image of continuity that allows him to forget nature's necessity. Wolmar's beneficence is a way of attaching others to himself through gratitude. He allows St. Preux into his household in order to confirm to himself that passionate love is nothing, and in order to secure the assistance of St. Preux in his old age. The attempt to cure St. Preux of his love for Julie is motivated less by his concern with St. Preux's happiness than with his own. Furthermore, Wolmar's wisdom is no more directed toward the common good than is his beneficence. His method for sincerity is not meant to form friendships as much as it is meant to guard St. Preux from the temptation to give into his love for Julie. And, his materialism, which cannot comprehend his own attachment to Julie, is used to reduce St. Preux's love to a matter of images derived from sense impressions. Both his beneficence and his wisdom are directed against the attachments between the lovers in order to subordinate them to his own needs.

Wolmar's attachments, like those of St. Preux, are also founded on illusions when seen from the perspective of reason. His greatest illusion is his attempt to overcome chance by becoming a god on earth. The psychological foundation for his household is the fear of death and the hope to relieve oneself from its terrors in the tenderness of marriage and the continuity promised by children. He believes that he is an atheist, whose mind is a mirror of necessity, and whose passions have been brought under its rule. Yet, his equanimity depends upon his imagination rather than his mind; he is of the opinion that he will die before his wife and children, when, in fact, the sequence of their deaths is a matter of chance rather than nature. Wolmar applies the regularity he sees in nature to the fates of individuals. When chance intervenes in his life and takes his wife from him, he comes to believe in God and the afterlife. Wolmar is no more successful than St. Preux in combining the generality of reason with personal attachments.

Given the conflict between love and family, and their conflict with nature and reason, the reader is inevitably led to wonder in what sense love and family can be considered a solution or alternative to the bourgeois. They are not strictly speaking solutions because they themselves are so problematic. Rousseau was fully aware of their problematic character, as is evident by the fact that he does not harmonize them with each other, or even with their essential elements. It is clear from the *Second Discourse* that primitive man remains a standard for civil man, and it is clear from the *Confessions* that the solitaire is more rational than the lover or the spouse. The problems are, therefore, more fundamental to Rousseau than any of the alternatives. But, the priority given to the problems over the possible solutions does not issue forth in a debilitated relativism. Rousseau clearly thinks that love and family are better and nobler than the bourgeois because they have integrity, both in the sense of having character and in the sense of integrating themselves into the whole. The bourgeois does not have integrity, in either sense of the term, because he is so divided between nature and society that he lacks the unity required for an opinion of himself and his place in relation to the animal and the divine. The conformism and materialism characteristic of bourgeois life is a way of forgetting the human situation by moving with the herd and by constricting oneself to the preservation and pleasures of the body. The bourgeois has no character because he has no self-knowledge and self-justification, and he has no awareness of the whole because he has no awareness of himself. He is a chaos, without any of the profundity and terror that can be associated with it; he is utterly lacking in nobility and happiness because he is nothing rather than something.

Although love and family are problematic, they are more worthy of choice than the bourgeois because they are more conducive to nobility and happiness. St. Preux's sacrifices and Wolmar's beneficence may have questionable motives and beliefs, but they are real acts that require the subordination of immediate interests, and which compel sympathy and admiration from the reader. These acts require character because they require the subordination of the self to a greater whole, and they require reflection about the whole and their place in it because societies containing order and union are necessarily accompanied by reflections on god and the afterlife. The reflections and actions of Wolmar and St. Preux contradict nature and reason, but they, nonetheless, confront the human situation more than does the bourgeois. Love and family are possibilities that try to face and solve the problem of sexual relatedness in light of the separateness caused by bodily pleasure and death. We cannot forget that Rousseau's criticisms against liberalism are directed against Locke's failure to find a union founded on intercourse and Hobbes' failure to make sense of preservation and society given the fact that of death.

Besides accompanying nobility and an awareness of the human situation, love and family are concerned with happiness. They are attempts to form agreeable lives by overcoming the incoherence of chaos and the finality of death. The bourgeois lives a disagreeable life because at one moment he indulges in sensual pleasures as if he were about to die, and, at the next moment, he builds and accumulates as if he had forever to live. His pleasures and sense of self have not been disciplined by an idea of death and eternity. Rousseau's romantic depiction of the beautiful makes possible an agreeable life because it allows the heart to speak. The beautiful lends esteem to sensuality and inner feeling to amour-propre. Thus, happiness, as well as nobility and character, require an integration into the whole.

Yet, it is not entirely clear how the fundamental problems relate to the virtue and happiness of human beings. Rousseau rejects the theoretical life and, therefore, the contemplation of the problems as a way to virtue and happiness. Yet, he also rejects the idea that the problems can be solved and, therefore, he does not abandon the standard of nature. He is somewhere between Plato and Nietzsche. The problems are historical accidents that can be scraped away to reveal an original natural wholeness. The wholeness required for character and happiness is not, therefore, provided by history or the will to power.

The question is whether Rousseau's discovery of nature is a true discovery, or whether it is the result of thinking through a theoretical position. Is his materialism a result of an experience of true being, or is it a result of reasoning through and directing his imagination by the dogmatic premise that man is by nature asocial? There is no doubt that his thinking through of materialism makes him more consistent than Lucretius, Hobbes, and Locke. But, he might be further from the truth by following an error to its furthest conclusion.

La Nouvelle Héloïse is written in conscious opposition to Plato. Rousseau replaces Socrates with Julie because personal relations require a bodily foundation, according to Rousseau, whereas, for Plato, they are formed around the soul. In the *Symposium*, Plato subordinates lovers to the unreciprocated love of truth, and, in the *Republic*, he subordinates the family to the requirements of wisdom. Rousseau replaces the philosopher with the female because he does not believe in the natural attraction toward knowledge, or the possibility of real friendships formed around the pursuit of it. The universality and atheism of reason are, for Rousseau, subordinate and derivative from the bodily sensations. The denial of the independence of reason, and the possibility of friendships founded on it, seems to be reductionistic, for it does not move in the direction of the first impressions or awareness of nature. The longing for a nobility and happiness that is shared with others and attaches oneself to them, is the surface from which one must begin and the direction in which one must move. Rousseau's materialistic foundation for personal attachments strikes me as reductionistic and dogmatic because it does not do full justice to the divine in man.

Bibliography

Aristotle. *Politics*. Trans. Lord. Chicago, 1984.

Bloom, Allan. *Politics and The Arts*. New York, 1960.

Hobbes, Thomas. *Leviathan*. Ed. Macpherson. New York, 1981.

Laclos, Choderlos de. 1987. *Les Liasons Dangereuses*. Trans. P. W. K. Stone. New York: Penguin Books.

Lorris, Guillaume. *The Romance of The Rose*. Trans. Harry W. Rob-bins. New York, 1962.

McDowell, Judith. *Julie or The New Eloise*. University Park, 1968.

Molière. 1959. *The Misanthrope*. In *The Misanthrope and Other Plays*. Trans. Wood. New York: Penguin Classics.

Muralt, Béat de. 1933. *Lettres sur les anglois et les francois*. Paris: H. Champion.

Nietzsche, Fredrich. *Beyond Good and Evil*. Trans. Kaufmann. New York, 1966.

Orwin, Clifford. "Rousseau and the Discovery of Political Compassion," in *The Legacy of Rousseau*. ed. Clifford Orwin and Nathan Tarcov, 1997 Chicago: University of Chicago Press.

Plato. *The Apology of Socrates*. Ed. Burnet. Oxford, 1986.

———. *Republic*. Trans. Bloom. New York, 1968.

Prévost, Antoine-François. *Manon Lescaut*. Trans. Tancock. New York, 1949.

———. *Memoirs of a Man of Honour*. New York, 1975.

Richardson, Samuel. *Clarissa*. Ed. Ross. New York, 1988.

Rousseau, Jean-Jacques. *Emile*. Trans. Bloom. New York, 1969.

———. *The First and Second Discourses*. Trans. Roger Masters and Judith Masters. New York, 1964.

———. *Julie ou La Nouvelle Héloïse*. Paris, 1964.

———. *Julie or The New Eloise*. Trans. and abridged by Judith H. McDowell. University Park, 1968.

———. *Letter to d'Alembert*. Trans. Bloom. New York, 1989.

———. *Narcisse*. Paris, 1964.

———. *On the Social Contract with Geneva Manuscript and Political Economy*. Trans. Judith R. Masters. Ed. Roger D. Masters. New York, 1978.

———. *The Reveries of the Solitary Walker*. Trans. Butterworth. New York, 1979.

Schwartz, Joel. *The Sexual Politics of Jean-Jacques Rousseau*. Chicago, 1986.

Shklar, Judith. *Men and Citizens: A Study of Rousseau's Social Theory*. Cambridge, 1969.

Starobinski, Jean. *Jean-Jacques Rousseau: Transparency and Ob-struction*. Trans. Goldhammer. Chicago, 1988.

Stendhal. *Chroniques italiennes*. Gallimard, 1952.

———. *Life of Rossini*. Trans. Calder. New York, 1985.

———. *On Love*. Trans. Sale. Bungay, 1984.

Tocqueville, Alexis de. *Democracy in America*. Trans. Lawrence. Ed. Mayer. New York, 1969.

Wollstonecraft, Mary. *A Vindication of the Rights of Women*. New York, 1992.

Index

About the Author

Mark Kremer is associate professor of political science and international affairs at Kennesaw State University. He has taught as Harvard University and Boston University, and is the author of *Apologies: Plato and Xenophon*.

CPSIA information can be obtained
at www.ICGtesting.com
Printed in the USA
LVHW040901301021
701972LV00004B/76